D0292335

The UNOFFICIAL Secret Diary of

Boris Johnson Aged 13¼

The UNOFFICIAL Secret Diary of Boris Johnson

Aged 13 ¼

Lucien Young

Quercus

First published in Great Britain in 2019 by

Quercus Editions Ltd
Carmelite House
50 Victoria Embankment
London EC4Y 0DZ

An Hachette UK company

Copyright © 2019 Lucien Young

The moral right of Lucien Young to be
identified as the author of this work has been
asserted in accordance with the
Copyright, Designs and Patents Act, 1988.

All rights reserved. No part of this publication
may be reproduced or transmitted in any form
or by any means, electronic or mechanical,
including photocopy, recording, or any
information storage and retrieval system,
without permission in writing from the publisher.

A CIP catalogue record for this book is available
from the British Library

HB ISBN 978 1 52940 664 1
Ebook ISBN 978 1 52940 666 5

Every effort has been made to contact copyright holders. However, the publishers will be
glad to rectify in future editions any inadvertent omissions brought to their attention.

Quercus Editions Ltd hereby exclude all liability to the extent permitted by law for any
errors or omissions in this book and for any loss, damage or expense (whether direct or
indirect) suffered by a third party relying on any information contained in this book.

10 9 8 7 6 5 4 3 2

Illustrations by Quinton Winter

Typeset by CC Book Production

Printed and bound in Great Britain by Clays Ltd, Elcograf S.p.A.

Papers used by Quercus are from well-managed forests and other responsible sources.

It is a tale

Told by an idiot, full of sound and fury

Signifying nothing.

– William Shakespeare, *Macbeth* (Act V, Scene 5)

Maximus bullshittus loquere

– The Johnson family motto

My SELF PORTRAIT

Messed up hair, to lull opponents into false sense of security ↓

Finely shaped skull, containing huge brain ↙

the chiselled physique of an Adonis →

Fingers crossed behind back.

Frankly magnificent calves →

All perfectly normal. Above average, if anything.

Foreword

Living, as we do, in increasingly strange times, it is only natural to look at our leaders and ask: 'what the hell is wrong with them?' Who are these rich aliens that hold our futures in their clammy hands? What motivates their cruel and seemingly arbitrary decisions? And, if we can just gain an insight into their minds, can we avoid the horrors they plan for us?

As a psychologist specialising in the thought processes of powerful individuals, I am often called upon to provide forewords for works touching on my field. However, it is fair to say that I have never contributed to a book quite like this.

What happened was this: on the 23rd July 2019, Boris Johnson had been elected leader of the Conservative Party, beating Jeremy Hunt (the man who launched a thousand Freudian slips). The following day, Johnson was appointed Prime Minister by Her Majesty the Queen. More importantly for our purposes, a removal van arrived at the

Camberwell flat Johnson shared with his girlfriend. With the UK being in the midst of a sweltering heatwave, it is perhaps understandable that a box of personal effects was dropped, causing its contents to scatter across the baking-hot pavement. No doubt blinded by intense sunlight, the movers failed to notice that one item had slid under a blue Škoda Superb, where it would remain until discovered by a passerby and sold to the publisher Quercus. It was no less than the teenage diary of our new Prime Minister.

Lucien Young – until then a struggling comedy writer – edited the volume, removing the inevitable schoolboy typos, and changing names where anonymity was required. He transcribed each entry, adding facsimiles of the various notes, doodles and documents found in the original diary. Thus the book you are currently holding came to be.

So what do the coming pages tell us about Alexander Boris de Pfeffel Johnson? The first thing that jumps out is how similar the boy was to the man. His all-consuming ambition is matched only by his unwillingness to put in the corresponding work. He lies constantly, often for no discernible reason (beyond, perhaps, his own amusement). The adolescent Boris's attitude towards women is particularly fascinating: they barely exist, except as a status symbol. He wishes to conquer and possess them, not out of boyish lust, but rather as a means to impress other males.

However, the insights this book offers are not limited to one tousle-haired sociopath. It also illustrates the unique and bizarre psychological environment of Eton, an elite British boarding school. When one removes a boy from his family and deposits him in a brutal, inescapable social hierarchy, considerable trauma ensues. In this hyper-masculine atmosphere, the Etonian knows that any weak point, including basic sincerity, can and will be attacked. Thus they often construct a persona as a means of self-defence, a way to hold the world at arm's length. In extreme cases, a boy will cultivate so successful a persona that it swallows up his original personality.

Boris is the ultimate Old Etonian. Since school, he has wielded bravado as a weapon, taking his anger, his insecurity and his will to power, then dressing them up as a big Wodehousian joke. Even when the joke stops being funny, he will persist in telling it, because the joke is all he has. Can *The Secret Diary of Boris Johnson, Aged 13¼* help us anticipate what his premiership holds in store? In this psychologist's opinion, I'm afraid not. One may diagnose a narcissist, but it is quite another thing to predict how their

3

condition will manifest. Given the present turmoil, and the innumerable challenges our nation faces in the modern world, it is practically impossible to say how this Prime Minister will bear up. As we hurtle towards Brexit, only one thing is for sure: whatever Boris Johnson cares about, it isn't us.

Dr Josephine Boe
Oxford
5th August 2019

1

MICHAELMAS

CHAPTER ONE

Floreat Etona!

Eton College, Berkshire.
Friday, 9th September

Dear Diary,

Salutations, greetings, howdy and an abundant wotcha! It is I, your owner: Alexander Boris de Pfeffel Johnson. Al, I hear you cry, what has compelled you to take up the diarist's pen? Well, two weeks ago I arrived to take up studies at the august and storied Eton College. Eton, it is agreed universally, represents the snow-capped apex of the British educational system. From its halls have emerged Nobel Prize winners, members of the Royal Family, and no fewer than eighteen Prime Ministers. With that in mind, it has occurred to me that I – young Alex Johnson – must be destined to join the ranks of Great Men. Hence I've decided to keep a diary, to give future historians something to pore over. I look forward to recording my many adventures and triumphs in these pages, dear D. We are forced to attend such tedious classes as Geography, Mathematics and R.E., so I shall have ample opportunity to update you.

Not much to report from today. I am writing this in my bare, narrow room, whose walls are enlivened only by a poster of Farrah Fawcett, which I purchased for the astronomical sum of two pounds. Spam fritters for lunch again. Every time they serve this, a violent uprising becomes more likely. After lights out, used torch to check my *mons pubis* for hair. Still nothing . . .

There was a young scholar named Boris
Whose wit outstripped Pliny and Horace
His vocab was vast
And greatly surpassed
The words within Roget's Thesaurus.

Saturday, 10th September

In the showers this morning, it occurred to me that, while I'm confident my fate is to be a Great Man, I'm not at all sure in what direction this greatness lies. Literature? The army?

Something dreary, like politics? Ah well, I suppose that's why one goes to Eton: to find out what you'll be in charge of. When I was but a wee nipper, I would often declare my intention to become 'World King'. While that position may not, strictly speaking, exist, you have to admire young Alex's spirit. Ultimately, what I do with my life doesn't really matter, so long as I end up at the top of the pile.

Did my daily groin check. The *m.p.* remains empty.

Sunday, 11th September

What can one say about Eton? It is a vision of stained glass and old stone, sitting just across the Thames from Windsor Castle, whose towers are visible from my window. Its massive courtyard contains a bronze statue of the founder, King Henry VI, and opposite the library is a cannon captured during the Crimean War. The occasional jumbo jet buzzes overhead on its way to Heathrow. Slough is nearby, but that can't be helped.

The school was originally founded to educate 'seventy poor and needy scholars', but fortunately we get a better sort these days. Its population consists of roughly a thousand boys. These are the sons of bankers, landed gentry and the

occasional foreign king. Our College motto is *Floreat Etona*, or 'may Eton flourish'. I think this is depressingly weedy, especially considering all the great Latin phrases out there. If it were up to me, I'd choose a quote from Lucius Accius: *oderint dum metuant* ('let them hate, so long as they fear'). The townsfolk of Windsor seem to have the hate part down, given the things they shout whenever one walks along the medieval high street in one's three-piece tail suit.

If these oiks were smart, they would put more emphasis on the fear. After all, we Etonians will one day assume the role of their lords and masters. This essential fact is constantly drilled into us: the walls are lined with busts of illustrious alumni. On our very first day, the Provost gave us a rather stirring speech. He told us we were Britain's future leaders, that we had a responsibility and a destiny that was not to be taken lightly. We were privileged, but we were also duty-bound to give back to society and contribute to it. I liked the first part, about us being special, though I rather lost interest when he got started on society.

It's only been a fortnight, but I'd say I've taken to Eton life like a duck to water (a handsome and impressive duck at that). The only thing with which I'm not yet comfortable is the uniform. I am forever being upbraided by the Dame for scruffiness.* I mean, who has the time to always tighten their tie, tuck in their shirt tails, wear trousers, etc.? Even worse, as a King's Scholar, I am compelled to go about in a massive, billowing gown, also known as a 'tug'. Everything here is called something else: terms are 'halves', teachers are 'beaks', and an hour of excruciating torture is called R.E. Prefects are known as 'praepostors', which strikes me as quite praepostor-ous (ha ha ha!). The purpose of all these code words is to stop any of the wrong sort slipping in.

A note on friends: one sees a lot of new bugs going about the place, requesting games of conkers, offering to share their tuck, etc. Their desperation to find a companion is palpable. Indeed, grown-ups tell anyone who'll listen that the most important part of school is the friendships you make. Well, I intend to remain aloof from all that. What's the point of blabbing one's secrets to someone, then having to feign interest as they drone on about their childhood trips to Cromer? There are far more efficient ways to influence people, such as intimidation and blackmail.

I suppose the closest thing I have to a confidante is a

---

* *Editor's note*: 'Dame' is the Eton term for matron.

12

fellow first year, labouring under the inauspicious name of Dominic Jessop-Jenkins. Dom is a frightful weed, and painfully eager to impress me, but he nonetheless has his uses. If I express a desire for toast, he will go scrambling to fetch it, and when I need to clean my rugby boots, he is more than willing to lend his jumper. Maybe friendship isn't so bad . . .

GUIDE TO COLLEGE SLANG

Beaks = Teachers

New bugs = First years

Aardvark = 50p coin (e.g. 'I'll give you two aardvarks for that copy of *Readers' Wives*.')

Winklevoss = Housemaster

Fag = A new bug that must act as servant to an older boy

Gollup = Another word for fag

Smokey Lionel = Fag (as in cigarette)

Blenko = Friend

Trunt = Homework

Gramsci's Neurotic Kitten = Toilet

Illustrative Dialogue

CLEVER ETONIAN: I say, blenko, the Winklevoss just fined me an aardvark for having a smokey Lionel in Gramsci's Neurotic Kitten!

IDIOT WHO DIDN'T GO TO ETON: You what, mate?

Monday, 12th September

A regrettably prominent part of the school experience is teachers. I have no problem with teachers, up to a point, and that point is when they start giving me work to do. Which is not to issue a blanket condemnation of all beaks. They inhabit a spectrum, ranging from 'not entirely hateful' to 'makes Attila the Hun seem like your old gran'. Occupying the former part of the spectrum is my Housemaster, Mr Parham. He is a twinkly-eyed sort, with a wry sense of humour. Unusually, he seems to enjoy the parts of his job that don't involve caning. He's also a Classics teacher – my favourite subject – so is able to direct me to the Greco-Roman texts with the most gore and incest.

Alas, today I had an encounter with the other sort of beak. I was mucking about in the cloisters, rolling marbles in front of boys as they scuttled from class to class. Before I had the chance to cause even a minor injury, I felt something grip my gown and yank me backwards. My worst suspicions were confirmed as I turned to take in the vulture-like visage of Mr A.R.F. Crighton. Old Crighty, as he's known, is a Maths teacher, Deputy Head and noted cane enthusiast.

'Johnson,' he thundered, 'what on earth do you think you're doing?'

I assumed my most convincing expression of beatific innocence.

'Why, sir, I was enjoying a swift game of marbles, as a palate cleanser before Physics. You know what they say: all work and no play makes Jack a dull boy.'

He wrinkled his nose, making him look even more vulture-ish than before. I suppose it makes sense that a beak should remind one of a bird.

'Be very careful, boy. I know that some here find your antics amusing, but I can assure you I am wholly immune.' With that he stomped off, or at least would have, had he not slipped on a stray marble. This resulted in a hundred lines for young Alex, but, on balance, it was worth it. How many opportunities does one get to see a vulture go arse over tit?

Checked the pubic mound once more before bedtime. No joy. It reminded me of a word I just discovered in the dictionary: *glabrous, noun – smoothly hairless, in the manner of a baby's bottom* . . .

I know of a blighter named Crighton
Whose words never serve to enlighten.
No offence to the guy,
But, if he should die,.
Then, Lord, how my prospects would brighten!

Thursday, 15th September

Today saw a regrettable incident. I fancied some toast
and jam, so burst into Jessop-Jenkins's room to demand
he make it. What I beheld inside shocked me to my very
marrow. He was not masturbating or attempting congress
with a barnyard animal – either of those scenarios I could
have met with sangfroid. No, Dominic's face was pink and
streaked with tears, a fact he vainly tried to conceal by
lifting his bed sheets.

'Good lord, man!' I exclaimed. 'Have you been blubbing?'

He dabbed at his big red eyes, sniffing wretchedly.

'Please don't tell anyone. It's just, we had that apple pie
at lunch, and it reminded me of how I used to go apple
picking with Mama and Papa. I . . . I miss them, is all.'

Naturally, my response was scathing. I pointed out that

he was being a wimp, a wet and a cowardy custard, and that the rest of school would be notified forthwith. Of course, this only intensified his blubbing, but it was for his own good.

In this place, one must put on a tough front at all times. Act brave, even if you're blubbing on the inside. A great many Etonians miss their parents. They can often feel abandoned, unloved, cast into a howling void of loneliness, where they must swiftly erect a defensive wall of bluster and bravado just to survive. Not me, though. I genuinely don't care one bit, and if anyone says I do, I shall duff them up with extreme prejudice.

Friday, 16th September

Said something frightfully witty in English. Mr Fortescue, our teacher and the bearer of an unfortunate lisp, asked me to define the word 'suffix', to which I responded: 'Why, Suffix is a county south of Effix.' The uproarious response from my classmates fully justified the lines I was given.

Mons watch '77: still no hair.

Saturday, 17th September

The low point of my Eton career so far. While rounding a corner into the courtyard, I collided with the muscular figure of Piers Davenant, President of Pop.* The bloke barely budged, while I was hurled to the ground. In my defence, I am a tender thirteen years old (though admittedly well developed), whereas Davenant is seventeen. I glanced up at my social superior: unrepentantly tall, with the sort of face that I suppose an undiscerning female might deem attractive.

As I got to my feet, I was alarmed to see that a crowd of boys had gathered.

'I say,' Davenant growled, 'new bugs should bloody well watch where they're going. You scuffed my shoes.'

'I–I'm terribly sorry,' I stammered.

'"I'm terribly sorry,"' he repeated, in a high-pitched parody of my voice that amused his audience no end. 'What

---

* *Editor's note*: 'Pop', more properly known as the Eton Society, is a self-selected group of the most popular boys at school, operating with full permission of the teaching staff. Members of Pop are given special privileges, such as the right to wear brightly coloured waistcoats. Again, these are the people in charge of our country.

19

a wuss! Look at that hair – combed within an inch of its life. You've parted it like Jesus did the Red Sea.'

I frowned.

'Actually, it was Moses who parted the Red Sea.'

'Ooh la la!' cried Davenant. 'Are you some kind of swot?'

At this, he grabbed my tug and gave it a violent yank.

'Oh, but of course you are – you're a Colleger. What's the matter, couldn't your father afford the fees?'

'I say, it's not my fault I did well in the exams!' This came out several octaves higher than I would have liked. Suddenly, Davenant's high-cheekboned face filled with recognition.

'Hang on, I know who you are. You're Alexander Johnson, that blighter who was born in New York and grew up in Brussels. What's more, I hear you're part bloody Turk.'

'Well, my great-grandfather was an Ottoman, but—'

'So tell me,' he continued, 'what are you doing here? This is an English school, for English gentlemen, not mutts from all over the place.'

I blushed as red as a tomato that had been caught with a dirty magazine. It struck me that some barbed rejoinder might save the situation, but all I could do was stare at my shoes. I mumbled some additional apologies and stalked off, the laughter of my fellow students echoing in my ears.

I spent the rest of the afternoon skulking around the playing fields, trying to avoid other boys. It is important to note, dear Diary, that I absolutely, categorically, one-hundred-per cent did NOT blub. Nonetheless, the Johnson mind was seething. How could I have allowed myself to be bested in this fashion? I had been made to look a fool by a more popular boy, and was quite sure that I would never recover from this humiliation. The rest of my time at Eton would be a joyless, brutal trudge, during which I would be spat upon by boy and beak alike. And the degradation wouldn't end there – the whole point of Eton is that these boys will always be around you. They will be your friends, your colleagues, your fellow cabinet ministers. Wherever I went, whatever I did, this altercation with Piers Davenant would hang around my neck like a decomposing albatross.

Yes, it's safe to say that your hero had taken a day trip to Gloomsville. However, you can't keep a good man down, and despair is the preserve of those less marvellous than me. I soon realised that this was not necessarily the end of the road. I could still redeem myself, win the esteem of my peers and conquer Eton as I had always planned to. However, to take on fellows like Davenant – handsome, sporty, naturally popular – I would need something new. An X factor. A way of speaking, of acting, of being. Something so extraordinary and outrageous that no one would ever be able to dismiss me again. I could no longer make do as weedy Alexander Johnson: I needed to become someone else. Sticking my hand in the neatly combed hair that Davenant had so harshly mocked, I ruffled it into a mad, exploded haystack, then headed back to my room.

Jessop-Jenkins was waiting there, sitting on my bed with a rather effeminate look of sympathy.

'Hullo Alex, old sport. I heard you had a run-in with Piers Davenant. What rotten luck! I hope you're all right.'

The last thing I needed was the platitudes of an established drip. I plopped onto the bed with a face like thunder.

'Why wouldn't I be all right? I've only been mocked and mortified in front of a decent-sized chunk of my cohort. If *you* know about it – a chap who's wetter than Niagara Falls – then so must everyone.'

Dominic placed what he must have imagined was a comforting hand on my shoulder.

'Everyone gets a ribbing from the older boys. You mustn't be so hard on yourself, Alex.'

Just then, a wave of hot rage arose in me.

'Stop calling me that!' I yelled. Jessop-Jenkins flinched, and so I added, in a somewhat gentler tone: 'Alexander is such a boring, ordinary name . . .'

His bovine features assumed a look of confusion.

'What shall I call you, then?'

I thought for a moment, then allowed myself a smile.

'Boris', I replied. 'Just Boris.'

UPDATE: checked the pubic region just now, only to find a magnificent golden thread! Perhaps today wasn't so bad after all. Watch out, world: Boris Johnson is here, and he's sprouting!

MY AVERAGE* DAY

07.00: Awake from dreams of world domination and un-limited Curlies Wurly. Make my ablutions, then update the extremely important historical text that is this diary. Spend at least quarter of an hour in front of the mirror, making sure my hair is unkempt in precisely the right way.

08.00: Breakfast. Reel at the inhuman vileness of school food. Yearn for something more delicious and nour-ishing, such as gravel.

08.35: Chapel. The Chaplain bangs on about Jesus, which I'm sure is terribly interesting if you're a fan of his. I amuse myself by imagining various scenarios, e.g. seducing Mary Magdalene, or having a beak crucified.

09.00: Lessons begin. Stave off boredom with secret pranks and pornographic doodling.

11.20: Break. A chance to gauge how the complex social hierarchy of the school has shifted since yesterday. I deploy some of the impromptu gags I prepared last night.

---

* Not that anything I do could be said to be average. A more accurate title would be 'My Wizzo, All-Conquering, Super-splendiferous Day'.

11.45: Yet more lessons. Look, I know these teachers need something to keep them occupied, but should we suffer as a result?

13.15: Lunch. The dinner ladies furnish us with some dish carefully selected from a wide range of inedible slop. There is much moaning and gnashing of teeth as we struggle to consume e.g. the wasp casserole without retching.

14.20: Activities. The activities the school has in mind are Duke of Edinburgh, cadets, etc. However, I often use this time to pursue my own activities (e.g. sowing discord/psychological warfare).

15.40: Sport. Of these, rugby's best, as it has the most scope to injure your opponent while plausibly maintaining that it was an accident.

18.15: Quiet hour, during which we're expected to sit around contemplating life, or scan an improving tome. Fat chance . . .

19.30: Dinner. Boys are forced back into the hall with cattle prods, there to receive another dose of salmonella. They fumble for their cyanide pills, desperate to escape the horror of a school meal, but these are soon confiscated.

20.15: Pretend to be doing private study/homework. In reality, continue to write my erotic thriller.

21.30: Lights out. Now the real fun begins.

21.45: Once content that the Housemaster is elsewhere, arrange dirty clothes under bed sheets to create decoy lump. This will not withstand real scrutiny, but may just give me the time I need to complete my mission.

22.00: Cavort and caper throughout the school, indulging in mischief, sabotage, etc. Perhaps take this chance to note down other boys' nocturnal escapades, for the purpose of future blackmail.

23.50: Gain ingress to the tuck shop by using lock-picking kit ordered from *Schoolboy Spy* magazine.

23.55: Raid tuck shop, escaping with plentiful Curly Wurlies (though not so many as to arouse suspicions come morning).

00.00: Midnight feast. Best enjoyed solo. Use the ensuing sugar rush to prepare tomorrow's witticisms, devise schemes, etc.

01.00: Crash from sugar high. Fall into the arms of Morpheus. Rinse and repeat.

CHAPTER TWO

Ad captandum vulgus

Sunday, 18th September

Today I discovered, to my infinite delight, that there is a place on Eton High Street named Porny School. Alas, it's a normal C of E primary, rather than, as the name would suggest, somewhere one learns to make blue movies.

Monday, 19th September

Saw Davenant and his cronies striding through the church yard, so leapt behind a low wall, landing face first on some recently deposited chewing gum. No matter. I now see such indignities as a boon – they will fuel my ascent to world dominance. Drawing inspiration from Richard Nixon, the last US President but one, I have decided to start keeping an enemies list.* This list goes as follows:

- Piers Davenant
- Assorted Davenant cronies
- Mr Crighton, aka Old Crighty
- My sis, Rachel (due to her disrespectful teasing)
- Every teacher and student at Ashdown House preparatory school
- Anyone who would even think of opposing my schemes
- Bruce Forsyth (I'm just not a fan)

Hmm, it strikes me that this list has the potential to become quite expansive. Perhaps it would make more sense to say that everyone is provisionally on my enemies list, until such time as they prove themselves loyal.

---

* Incidentally, what did Nixon *really* do wrong? The Watergate stuff seems terribly overblown to me. Why would the Democrats mind having their headquarters bugged unless they had something to hide? I think if a fellow insists to you that he's not a crook, one ought to take him at his word.

When one is a student of Eton
One knows one shall never be beaten.
One's path to success
Is quite frictionless;
The truth of this thing bears repeatin'.

Tuesday, 20th September

Had the most wondrous and educational experience today. During Latin this a.m., our teacher Mr Beesley – he of the confetti dandruff and bodily odours – demanded that I get up and give a brief talk on Catullus. Apparently I'd volunteered to do so last week, then forgotten about it entirely. Well, dearest D., I don't mind telling you that Boris's brain was mightily flummoxed.

Without the faintest clue what I was about to say, I rose to my feet.

'Um, gosh, yes, Catullus,' I began. 'What can one say about Catullus? Well, I have always strived to keep my feelings on Catullus a secret. But now I shall have to let the Cat-ullus out of the bag.' At this, the other boys began to chortle. In retrospect, I'm not sure what I said was actually *funny*, but one can generally get a laugh by being posh and confident and pulling a face.

'Yes, yes, very good, Johnson,' said Mr Beesley, 'but you're meant to be telling us about his poetry.'

'Well, um, quite,' I shot back. 'And I thank our greatly esteemed and, uh, fragrant *magister* for the chance to do so.' More chortles. I continued:

'Knowing, as I do, so much about Catullus – and, indeed, his poetry! – it's tough to know where to begin. Perhaps, then, I should start with the basics: Catullus was a Roman. As such, he had a Roman Head, roman shoulders and, of course, *Roman hands*. Yes, that poet's hands would roam all over the place. He was the most notorious bottom-pincher in the whole republic! In fact, I am reliably informed that no senator's wife was safe when randy Mr Catullus came round.' Yet more laughter!

I don't recall the rest of what I said, but it hardly matters. Warming to my theme, I puffed out my cheeks, messed up my hair, and began to gesticulate wildly. At random intervals, I threw out amusing words like 'gadzooks!' and 'crikey!' By this point, even old Beesley was chuckling away. I got off scot-free, with no lines or detention. Which just goes to show: being prepared or knowing about stuff is for the birds. Perhaps such nerdishness is useful to commoners and women, but not when you're Boris Johnson, the cleverest boy in the world!

MY HEROES
by

Boris Johnson

PART ONE

As a great Alexander myself, I've always had a soft spot for
the all-conquering Macedonian. He was tutored by Aristotle
until the age of sixteen, and – a testament to his tremendous
fortitude – managed not to die of boredom. At twenty, he

succeeded his father to the throne and decided to show the Persians who was boss.

By thirty, he had forged an empire that stretched from Greece to north-western India, which is not bad going. I might feel intimidated, if I didn't have seventeen years to catch up. Plutarch tells us that Alexander once wept over not having conquered the whole world, which is a bit weedy, but I'll forgive him this once.

Such grand heroes of antiquity appeal to me. I find myself identifying with your Alexanders, your Caesars, your Neros. These guys paid no heed to the whining plebs, or to teachers, or parents, or cavilling eggheads. They just went about, being great and posing for big, muscly statues. I wonder how many statues will be made of me . . .

Wednesday, 21st September

I have never been a proponent of exercise in any of its forms – it always seemed a distraction from more important endeavours, such as eating Curly Wurlies or lazing about – but I must admit that Eton has changed my mind on the subject. Sport, particularly rugby, is a central part of the public school experience, building, as it does, character, and encouraging, as it also does, manly virtues. What could better equip a young man for society than a game where one must inflict extreme violence on others in order to achieve one's objectives?

The crux of rugby is this: both teams get in a scrum, where they try, as subtly as possible, to injure their opponents. The ref blows his whistle, at which point the violence becomes overt. Players then proceed to headbutt, to strangle and to rake their studs across exposed shins, while everyone on the sideline bellows: 'Get into him!' There's a ball involved, but don't worry too much about that. Rugby has taught me a great deal about the importance of context. In most settings, to bodily slam a smaller boy, administer a few good kicks to the ribs, then sit on his head would be frowned upon. However, on the rugger pitch, it is actively encouraged.

I'm proud to say I'm something of a natural when it comes to the sport: my stout physique, low centre of gravity and total disregard for the welfare of others have all proved to be assets. Mr Dickens, the Games Master, was particularly complimentary about a rough tackle I perpetrated on the weedy form of Timothy Fitznigel. However, he did observe that I acted unconventionally, given Fitznigel wasn't holding the ball at the time. I can't say that the 'scoring tries' aspect of the game interests me much. The prime joy of these lessons is that you can commit GBH against a rival, and if he objects, you just dismiss him as unsportsmanlike.

There's one chap I wouldn't mess with on the field of rugby (or, indeed, anywhere else) and that is Adrian Bullard. Despite being two months younger than me, the guy has the build of a prizefighting gorilla, along with said creature's body hair and IQ. Watching him plough through the ranks of his adversaries, it became clear to me that here was someone I wanted on my side. In the

changing rooms afterwards, I gave Bullard a congratulatory Curly Wurly. I took his grunt of approbation to mean that he and I have reached an understanding.

Wednesday, 28th September

My faithful D.,

Apologies for my neglect of you this past week. It is quite intolerable, and I intend to make amends by tenderly stroking your pages and feeding you tonnes of delicious ink. The fact is, I've been busy, for Boris's social cachet has, of late, achieved hitherto unthinkable tumescence. It would seem that word of my class-clowning has spread, generating intense interest among the boys. Nowadays, people call out 'Boris, legend!' as I walk to Biology. I have even acquired something of an entourage, in the form of Ridgeley-Watts and Edge-Llewelyn, who sit with me at lunch, hanging on my every word. Jessop-Jenkins – bless his feeble heart – is clearly intimidated by all the new faces around yours truly. Earlier today, he admonished me to remember who my real pals were, namely 'the ones who supported you from the very beginning'. Of course, this is truly tragic, but I welcome it as a demonstration of how popular I have become. It is immensely gratifying to have such good . . . well, I wouldn't call them friends. They can more accurately be characterised as fans, acolytes, followers. I might even call them disciples, were that not inappropriate (none of these guys would betray me – bad luck, Jesus!).

Thursday, 29th September

At lunch, a rum occurrence. I was in hall, attempting to coax some leathery beef down my gullet, when I got an earful of the following:

'Sal si tibi placet.'

It was the poshest voice I'd ever heard, and, given my background, that's really saying something. I turned to see a tall, slender boy with an old-fashioned demeanour and grave features. All in all, he resembled the ghost of a Victorian undertaker.

'What was that?' I asked.

Annoyed at being made to repeat himself, he rolled his eyes elaborately.

'*Sal si tibi placet*. It's Latin for "please pass the salt". One would expect a fellow scholar of Eton to know that.'

Now, I mean, really . . . I count myself a prime devotee of the classical world, but there is a time and a place for Latin, and this was neither. Nonetheless, I handed him the salt.

'So what's your name, then?' I demanded.

'Rees-Mogg,' he drawled, 'Jacob William. Now, if you'll excuse me, I must return to my reading.'

With that, he marched back to his seat, where he picked up a book entitled *Self-flagellation Techniques of the Catholic Saints*. This is all quite disturbing. Here I was, thinking I had a monopoly on being eccentric at Eton, when suddenly this Rees-Mogg chap appears from the eighteenth century! I reckon he's a bit too weird and spooky to pose a threat, but shall keep an eye on him nonetheless.

Friday, 30th September

Was horrified when, at rugby today, I was viciously tackled from behind by Timothy Fitznigel. The rotter set me face

down into a mud puddle and damn near broke my (noble and impressive) nose. What could have possessed him to act so brutishly? I know I tackled him the other day, but that was light-hearted, cheeky, all a bit of fun. Doing the same to me is, quite frankly, unconscionable.

Saturday, 1st October

A pleasant daydream in History this morning: I imagined I was Vlad the Impaler, and had a grand old time mounting my enemies on spikes and swishing about in a large cape. 'Boris the Impaler' doesn't sound right, though. Boris the Perforator? Johnson the Jabber?

Exacted vengeance upon Timothy Fitznigel by entering his room around 2 a.m. and emptying a can of olive oil over his head, then a jar of coffee powder. Dashed out before he could identify his assailant, but took considerable pleasure in hearing Dim Tim's cries resound through the corridor.

Sunday, 2nd October

Mr Parham has instigated a large-scale investigation into last night's oiling and coffee-ing of Fitznigel. Less hardy souls might be alarmed by this, but I am confident that I shall evade the dragnet. After I had done the deed, I returned to my room and threw the empty can and coffee jar out the window. I then returned to the corridor – where a group of boys had been drawn by Fitznigel's yells – rubbing my eyes and feigning surprise. Thus evidence was disposed of, and an alibi established.

As such, I was able to maintain my composure when, like all the other boys in the house, I was called into Parham's study to account for my whereabouts that night. My saucer-like eyes brimmed with innocence, and I allowed my voice to quaver slightly as I pled my case:

'I think this whole business is ghastly, positively ghastly. If only I could provide some assistance in bringing the culprit to justice. Alas, that night saw me repair to bed early with an improving tome. I was fast asleep, dreaming of wholesome things, when I was woken by Fitznigel's caterwauls.'

Perhaps my speech was a little over-rehearsed, but I reckon it did the trick. Impatient, Parham tapped a pen against his notebook.

'Do you have any inkling who might have done this?'

'No, sir. I can't think why anyone would wish to cause Fitznigel upset.'

'He says that you and he recently clashed on the rugby field.'

I put on a show of astonishment.

'Oh, that? That was all fun and games. One mustn't take sporting scuffles to heart.'

I felt Mr Parham's gaze bore into me, and cold beads of sweat began to form on my back. When an octopus feels cornered on the ocean floor, it will shoot out a cloud of ink to confound its predators. I do much the same thing, except with words.

'Actually, sir, when I said I couldn't think why anyone would wish to cause him upset, that wasn't entirely true.'

'Oh?'

'It's not the sort of thing I like to bring up, but Fitznigel is – I'm afraid to say – not terribly popular with the other boys. You hear him described as a frog-faced simpleton and a fat, arrogant dildo – not my words, of course.'

There was a frosty pause before the Housemaster spoke again.

'Johnson, is there something you would like to tell me?'

'No, sir,' I replied. This time I was being honest.

I escaped Mr Parham's study, and was keen to return to my digs unaccosted. Alas, this was not to be. As I passed through the common room, I detected a pungent whiff of coffee and olive oil. I turned to see my victim sat in an armchair, his head shining in the light.

'Fitznigel,' I said. 'I love what you've done with your hair.'

'You toerag!' he exclaimed, leaping to his feet. 'I've taken five showers today and I still reek to high heaven.'

'To be fair,' I replied, 'that was true before last night.'

He advanced on my person, threateningly.

'I know it was you, Johnson. I may not be able to prove it, but I shall never forgive you.'

'You have no basis on which to blame me,' I scoffed. 'And, if I had done it, it would have been entirely justified by your appalling behaviour on the rugby field.'

Fitznigel squawked with indignation.

'*My* appalling behaviour? You started it by damn near breaking my ribs.'

I raised a dismissive hand:

'I'm not going to stand here and quibble about what may or may not have happened, and in which order. What does it matter? Honestly, Fitznigel, you're like one of those

Africans who rail against the British Empire, just because we did a bit of enslavement. Get over it!'

Fitznigel looked like he was about to hit me, and he might have done, were it not for a group of boys entering the common room. Among them were my associates Edge-Llewelyn, Ridgeley-Watts and Jessop-Jenkins.

'I say, Fitznigel,' said Edge-Llewelyn, 'lay off Boris.'

The group murmured its general assent that no harm should come to me.

'Why are you defending him?' asked a pained Fitznigel. 'He's a total snake. He would screw any of you over in a heartbeat.'

'Sure,' came the reply, 'he's a bit of a rotter, but he's a bloody good laugh.'

'So what?' cried Fitznigel. 'Just because he pulls the occasional face doesn't mean he gets to be a liar, a thug and a fraud!'

'It *does* mean that!' yelled Jessop-Jenkins, with surprising boldness. 'Now buzz off . . . olive-oil hair!'

It is a testament to herd mentality that this lame insult got such a laugh. Realising that there was no justice to be found, a teary Fitznigel retreated to his room. I must say I was mightily buoyed by this interaction – my faith in humanity is restored!

The BALLAD of BORIS the BRAVE

Come gather round, folks,
And I'll tell you the tale
Of a fellow called Boris,
Who never did fail.
This man was the rare sort
Of whom legend tells;
His brain was enormous,
As was something else.

Chorus:
Boris the mighty, Boris the great,
Boris the splendid, everyone's mate.
Boris the clever, starter of trends,
Boris beloved, haver of friends.

From prep school to Eton
Young Boris progressed
And lived every moment
With courage and zest
He never was wussy
And never felt sad.
"We're ever so proud"
Cried his Mum and Dad.

(Chorus)

The marvellous Boris
Outshone everybody,.
From Carter to Brezhnev
To Showaddywaddy.
"I seem such a bore,"
Howled the poor Dalai Lama,
"Compared to young Boris,
That golden-haired charmer!"

(Chorus, loud)

Of course there were fools
Who would stand in his way,
But their lot was nothing
Save tears and dismay:
For when the vast flag
Of his genius unfurled
Then all proclaimed Boris
The King of the World!

(Chorus, X3, at absolutely deafening volume)

Monday, 3rd October

Received the following missive from my sister (a 'sis-miss', if you will):

Dear AL (or is it 'Boris' now?),

Your beloved Rachel here, just checking in to make sure you're not getting too big-headed. I know it must be terribly exciting to find yourself at big boy school, but do bear in mind that you're still the fellow who cried for days when I dropped your teddy in the duck pond.

Remember when you used to march around the house, declaring yourself "World King" and calling the rest of us "bog-brained serfs"? No doubt your time at Eton has rid you of such megalomaniacal instincts, and you are now a hushed and dutiful scholar.

Anyway, no major news from the home front. Bertie has laryngitis, which isn't something I was aware a Labrador can get, but there you go. Hopefully he will bark lustily once more by the time you're home for Christmas. Until then, enjoy being Mr Eton, and try not to be too much of a dick.

Yours sororally
Rachel

What cheek! I shall respond to this once I have mustered an appropriate level of invective.

Tuesday, 4th October

I must admit, I have been rather unsettled the past couple of days, with the Fitznigel investigation hanging over me like Damocles' sword. However, the 'heat', as they call it in American gangster films, has now died down. Mr Parham seems to have accepted that there is nothing he can do, beyond more patrolling of the corridors at night and frequent room inspections by Prefects. That suits me down to the ground, as it will make it harder for Fitznigel to take any retaliatory measures. They say there's no such thing as the perfect crime, but when I catch a glimpse of Timothy's still-glistening bonce, I'm inclined to disagree.

Thursday, 6th October

I was sequestered in my room, 'studying', when the door was troubled by the faintest of knocks.

'Enter,' I sighed. In crept Jessop-Jenkins.

'Afternoon, Boris. I'm afraid Mr Parham would like to

see you in his study . . .' The poor fellow was shaking like a leaf – clearly he feared, on some subconscious level, that the trouble I was in might be catching.

As I plodded towards Parham's study, my thoughts naturally turned to *l'affaire Fitznigel*. Had the school authorities located the olive oil can and coffee jar, then sent them off to be dusted for fingerprints? Was I to be rusticated, or even sent down – my Eton career over before it could be said to have begun? Mr Parham was not giving anything away. I entered his room to find him stoically puffing on his pipe.

'Ah, Johnson, do take a seat.'

I dragged my heavy feet across the room, as though approaching the guillotine.

'Sir, if this is about Fitznigel—'

'No,' said Sir. 'I wanted to talk about your essay on Ovid's *Metamorphoses*.'

My heart, which had been using my mouth as a holiday home, now returned to its regular gaff. Parham brandished a piece of paper, covered in spidery scrawl.

'I'm afraid this latest effort falls short of the standard we expect of a scholar. It seems rather as though you tossed it off at the last moment, using a thesaurus to bulk out your word count.'

48

'Sir,' I protested, 'that is absurd, crazy, goofy, illogical, laughable, ludicrous, nonsensical, preposterous and silly!'

In truth, the essay had been a rush job. In the run-up to the deadline, I had been preoccupied with my favourite comic book, *Rex Radium, Lord of Zargatron*, and so was forced to bash the thing out fifteen minutes before it was due. I bow to no one in my admiration of Ovid, but tentacled fiends and twelve-breasted space maidens must take precedence.

Nevertheless, one doesn't like to have one's academic prowess impugned. For whatever reason, I would like Mr Parham to think well of me, so I decided that theatrics were called for. Wibbling my lower lip and wringing tears from my eyeballs, I got to work:

'I'm s-s-sorry, sir. You're right – I've been distracted. Th–the thing is, my beloved dog Bertie is ill. It's quite serious, I'm afraid – the vet says he only has a . . . fifteen per cent chance of survival. I promised myself I wouldn't let the grief affect my schoolwork – that's not what Bertie would want – but clearly I've failed.'

I confess I was proud of this fabrication. Like all the best lies, it combined an element of truth with complete fantasy. Plus, it is a gift that will keep giving – when, inevitably, I find myself in the stew again, I can always kill Bertie off. Parham regarded me levelly, then drew on his pipe.

'I shall let you off this once, but any further slapdash efforts will be met with punishment. Please do not forget what a privilege it is to be at this school and benefit from its many resources.'

Here he regarded me with a tinge of sadness.

'Everyone knows you're clever, Johnson. I just hope you're not becoming complacent.'

What absolute rot! How could I possibly become complacent when I'm so very smart? I darted out of the study and put the unpleasant experience behind me by returning to the delights of Planet Zargatron.

CHAPTER THREE

Dulce est desipere in loco

Monday, 10th October

I seem, dear Diary, to have become something of a star. Boys swarm around me, eager to hear my latest witticism, or for me to do a disparaging impression of Mr Crighton. For the first time I can recall, I'm never on my own – whether it's Jessop-Jenkins, Edge-Llewelyn, Tukes, Unsworth or Ridgeley-Watts, there's always someone poking their head round my door. They want a piece of Boris, and that's absolutely, positively, stonkingly A-okay with me. After all, what's the point of doing anything if you don't have an audience?

My first month at England's finest school has taught me something vital: the importance of acting the fool. You should come across as a buffoon one moment, then whip-smart the next. This policy has two highly desirable results: firstly, it allows you to keep everyone's expectations nicely off-kilter. Secondly, it ensures that other boys won't resent you as a clever clogs. The key is to always seem nonchalant.* Even your most painstaking endeavours should appear casual – *sprezzatura*, as the Eyeties call it.

Every evening now, following lights out, I hunker down beneath the duvet, my trusty mini torch clenched between my teeth. In an A5 notepad, I map out the next day's off-the-cuff remarks and spur-of-the-moment stunts. Perhaps I will wave a kipper about in Chemistry. Or hoist my underwear on the school flagpole. The main thing is keeping the Boris show on the road.

Tuesday, 25th October

Dear Diary,

A million billion *quadrillion* apologies for my inattention these last few weeks. I know I'm no Samuel Pepys – in fact, you've barely heard a Samuel Peep from me. So what's been going on? In the words of that Etonian PM Harold

---

* Incidentally, can one be 'chalant'? Or is that like being 'whelmed' or 'gruntled'?

'Supermac' Macmillan: 'events, dear boy, events'. My popularity among the studentry has continued to skyrocket. Everyone wants me to join their club, and I oblige them, be it chess, aviation, fencing, magic, opera, climbing, sailing, wine tasting or philately. Hell, I'm a member of both the Atheist Society and Opus Dei. Any excuse to bask in some warm, gooey attention.

Meanwhile, the beaks are forever pecking at me, insisting I need to focus on essays, etc. Don't they know the social side of Eton is a full-time job? Expecting us to do schoolwork seems cruel and unusual. The upshot of all this is that my diary-keeping has been spottier than Jessop-Jenkins (if I haven't mentioned the blighter's acne, that's because it's only his twelfth most objectionable feature). However, this state of affairs must now change. My ascent to the highest echelons of Etonian society has made it even more clear that I was born to be a leader of men. And presumably women too, for what it's worth. Hence I recommit to chronicling these, my formative years. I vow, by all that is sacred, to pen a new entry every single night. Unless I'm too tired or had a big dinner or something. I'm only human, goddammit!

Wednesday, 26th October

Finally got round to replying to that impudent letter from my sister Rachel. I began with a list of my already considerable achievements at Eton, before indulging in a comprehensive demolition of her personality and appearance. I can't be bothered to transcribe the whole thing here, but rest assured it was as belletristic as it was trenchant. Particularly cutting sections included one in which I call Rachel a 'veritable smorgasbord of mediocrity', and one referring to her as a 'big stinky poo-poo head'. Hey, sometimes erudition must take a back seat to passion. In any case, she'll think twice before teasing me again.

Monday, 31st October

After nearly two months at Eton, I thought I knew every boy in my year. However, I made a new and unwelcome acquaintance today. I had entered the tuck shop, looking to stock up on CWs, when I was told, to my horror, that they were fresh out. Old Mrs Oliphant said: 'Oi'm sarry, Masturr Boris, but thart young gentullmun took the larst wun.' She indicated another boy, drifting towards the exit.

I followed the cove out into the street. He was younger than me, with wavy, brown hair, apple-red cheeks and a lordly attitude. Despite being a tiny little chap, he had an air of complete, unthinking confidence, eyeing the ancient stones of Eton as though he owned the place. Clearly this guy had been born with a silver spoon in every orifice. I intercepted him, taking a firm but reasonable tone.

'I say, excuse me. You might not have heard this, but I'm pretty much the Curly Wurly guy at school. If there's only one left, an unspoken agreement says it goes to me.'

'Really?' came his languid reply. 'I had no idea.'

'Not to worry,' I said, with magnanimity. 'You weren't to know. There are so many rules in this place – it can be overwhelming.'

'Oh, I wouldn't say that. All seems fairly straightforward to me. Plus, I had a preview. My older brother's here, a few years ahead – Alexander Cameron.'

'Ah,' I said, 'so you're Cameron Minor.'

He replied: 'Please, call me Dave.'

I told him he could call me Boris, and requested – again, quite firmly and reasonably – that he hand over the Curly Wurly. He responded by tearing the wrapper and taking an insouciant bite. Naturally, I saw red.

'Now, listen here, "Dave",' I spat, 'you might want to watch yourself. I'm something of a big shot around these parts.'

A scintilla of a condescending smirk played across Cameron's face.

'Oh yes? I was under the impression that true big shots don't have to tell people they're big shots.'

With that, he turned on his heel and shimmered off, chomping a Curly Wurly that was mine by rights. As I watched his aristocratic arse vamoose, I found myself thinking that, if I should ever find myself in a position to thwart and destroy this Cameron, I would assuredly do so. After all, if there's one thing I hate, it's unearned confidence.

There was a young fellow of Windsor
Who got his cock caught in a mincer.
His wife was tight-lipped
As he swore that he'd slipped,
But nothing he said could convince her.

Thursday, 10th November

Another letter from that accursed sister of mine:

Dear Boz-Boz,

Many thanks for your recent letter. Despite the rather pitiful attempts to put me down, I was nonetheless entertained by your many spelling mistakes and grammatical errors.

I was also tickled by what you call your 'Litany of achievements thus far'. Popularity, dear Boris, is fleeting, and all these double-barrel-types following you about sound like utter goons. As for your newfound reputation as school wit, well, you'll forgive me if I'm not exactly blown away. Fine, you've managed to elicit some giggles at the expense of teacher — so what? Every class in every school in the land contains some show-off, desperate to offset their personality deficit with attention. Don't let that stuff turn your head.

Home remains a vacuum of anything interesting. You will be pleased to learn that Bertie has recovered from his laryngitis and, delighted to find this faculty restored, is now basking from dawn till dusk. In fact, he seems even more taken with his own voice than you!

Yours epistolarily
Rachel

As provocative as her last! I must take some time to fully consider my revenge. In the words of King Lear, I'm not sure what actions I'll settle on, but they shall be the terrors of the thingie.

THINGS I SAY	WHAT I MEAN
'You raise an excellent point.'	I wish to God you hadn't brought that up.
'If I could just chime in . . .'	Stop talking, you bog-brained serf.
'Ah yes, I've been looking for you.'	I spent the last fifteen minutes in a cupboard, praying you would leave.
'I'm afraid that was my last Curly Wurly.'	It'll be a cold day in hell before I let you near my stash.
'No hard feelings.'	I shall see you die bloodily.
'I take full responsibility.'	. . . for the crimes you know about.
'Mr Crighton is tough but fair.'	When I take charge, Old Crighty is first up against the wall.
'Thanks for correcting me.'	Die. Die now.
'Bullard is quite the character.'	i.e. Mr Hyde.
'You can count on me.'	. . . to comprehensively screw you over.

Friday, 25th November

Due to his much-lauded articulacy, A.B.P. Johnson, Esq. has been selected to deliver the end of term speech. This is considered a great honour, and means speaking in front of the whole school. Alas, what excitement I might have felt at the prospect was obliterated by the speech I was given. I had hoped it would be something juicy, like Henry before Agincourt, or one of those Hitler ones where he's windmilling his arms about. Instead, it's a yawn-inducing piece by some dreary clergyman, entitled 'The Virtue of Diligence' or 'The Diligence of Virtue' or something of that nature. Here is a representative passage:

*The ideal boy is, at bottom, considerate, humble and honourable. He is motivated neither by burnished trophies nor loud acclaim; for him, the quiet satisfaction of a job well done is reward enough. A good boy is also a clean boy: clean not just in the sense of hygiene, but also his conduct and outlook. As Juvenal puts it in his tenth Satire, '*mens sana in corpore sano*' – a healthy mind in a healthy body.*

And on and on it goes. Well, yah boo sucks to that! What the Revd Algernon Brundish evidently fails to grasp is that this ideal boy of his is a drip and a dullard. More pressingly, I shudder to think how my social stock will tumble when I have to get up and say this tripe . . .

Friday, 9th December

I awoke on this, the day of my big speech, with a profound sense of dread. I had given my compeers every reason to believe that I was a maverick, a rebel, a loose cannon with a live wire. Now I was going to get up in front of them and parrot the words of some Victorian vicar. What damage might that do to the persona I'd worked so hard to cultivate? Would the Boris brand be fatally compromised by this display of obsequiousness, submission and teacher's-pet-ery?

I was entering the assembly hall, weighed down with such thoughts, when Mr Crighton, everyone's least favourite disciplinarian, approached.

'I shall be watching your speech very carefully, Johnson,' he growled. 'Be aware that any deviation from the approved script will be punished.'

At this point, he shot an involuntary glance towards the

Headmaster, leaving me in no doubt why he was so eager for things to go smoothly.

I assumed a seat by the side of the stage, nervously folding and unfolding my notes. After an eternity which lasted about five minutes, the Head Man got up and began to address the gathered boys. We heard that it had been an excellent Michaelmas, that we boys could be proud of our contributions to school life, and that this standard should be maintained through Lent. Then came the fearful words: 'Now, to read the end of term speech, please welcome Boris Johnson.'

As I took to the stage, I could hear a general murmur of anticipation. I gazed out at the crowd. There were Tukes, Bullard, Ridgeley-Watts and Jessop-Jenkins, all expecting me to be the character I had created: brave, bold, bombastic Boris. I cleared my throat and began.

'As John Wesley observed in 1778, cleanliness is next to godliness. These are wise words, which the virtuous schoolboy would do well to take to heart . . .'

After a few such lines, the excited whispers fell silent. By the second paragraph, they were replaced by groans. The sound of restless buttocks shifting in their seats was all but deafening. I had lost my audience, but what could I do? I ploughed on.

'The ideal boy is, at bottom, considerate, humble and honourable.'

Just then, a light bulb appeared above my head.

'At bottom,' I repeated. 'At . . . bottom . . . That's a strange choice of words, isn't it?'

As soon as I started to extemporise, a sharp cough issued from the crowd. Mr Crighton leaned forwards in his chair, doubtless wishing he could fire death rays in my direction. However, his ire was accompanied by a smattering of giggles.

'If you ask me,' I continued, 'it's a little odd that this clergyman was so preoccupied with what boys are like "at bottom". As far as I'm concerned, young boys' bottoms should be left alone. But our esteemed teachers clearly disagree, or they wouldn't be making me read this.'

The giggles now mutated into full-blown laughter. I glanced again at Old Crighty, on whose face a network of roseate veins was pulsating.

'Sorry, I should return to the text as written . . . A good boy is also a clean boy: clean not just in the sense of hygiene, but also his conduct and outlook. As Juvenal puts it in his tenth *Satire*, *"mens sana in corpore sano"*.'

I paused once more, contorting my features in a look of kabuki-style bafflement.

'*Mens sana* . . . What's that about a men's sauna? God knows what they get up to in there, given all the steam. Sounds rather dirty to me . . .'

Yet more laughter. I then proceeded to spill my notes across the floor, and made an elaborate pantomime of gathering them up, knocking over the lectern in the process. Boys whooped and cheered in response. It was at this point that I was scooped up by Mr Crighton and hauled offstage.

'You've made a big mistake,' he hissed in my ear, but the receding cheers told a different tale. I could even hear a chant beginning: 'BO-RIS! BO-RIS! BO-RIS!'

Looking back, I don't regret my decision to go off-piste and play the speech for laughs. My head and heart tell me it was the right call. My bottom, however, offers a dissenting opinion. That bastard Crighton wasn't lying re punishment, and he was zealous in his application of the cane. I'll admit I'm struggling to write this, due to the profusion of pink welts across my nether regions, which make sitting at my desk a Herculean task.

Saturday, 10th December

Backside still in tatters. Cannot justify time at writing desk.

Sunday, 11th December

Arse pain remains excruciating. However, I am comforted by the steady stream of boys visiting my room to tell me my speech was the funniest thing they had ever seen. If the price I must pay for such reverence is the integrity of my rump, then I pay it gladly.

Wednesday, 14th December

End of term meeting with Mr Parham constituted a one-man good cop, bad cop routine. He opened by remarking that I'm a bright, exceptionally eloquent boy, who has the potential to be a credit to the school. Then the good cop's less amiable colleague made himself known. Apparently my behaviour and general attitude are a cause for concern, and my numerous vices threaten to eclipse what virtues I possess.

'Boris,' said Mr Parham, 'I hope you will think about your behaviour over Christmas and come back with a better attitude in the New Year. You're an ambitious chap, and that can be commendable. But ambition on its own is not enough. What counts is the steady, unglamorous work that goes into doing anything worthwhile.'

He kept on in this vein for approximately ten minutes, while I drifted into a reverie about what Christmas presents I would receive in an ideal world (Gatling gun, grenades, TNT with attached plunger). Tomorrow I shall be heading home for the holidays, there to bask in the affection and admiration of my relatives. I can hear their voices now: 'Oh Al, our lives have been grey and pointless without you', 'My, how big your muscles have become', 'Who's a gorgeous genius, then?', etc. etc. Frankly, I could do without all that hogwash. I would much rather stay here and continue my progress towards conquering Eton (the first step to world domination).

ETON COLLEGE
SCHOOL REPORT

STUDENT NAME: Boris Johnson   **HALF:** Michaelmas

As Boris' House Master, I am pleased to report that your
son is taking to Eton life with gusto. He is keenly aware
of the school's many opportunities to mark oneself out with
achievements. Indeed, some might accuse him of a surfeit of
competitive spirit. He is already known on the rugby field
as a formidable and injurious opponent, and has lustily
pursued a spot in the choir, despite the fact his voice
only excels in volume. Furthermore, he seems genuinely
baffled to have not yet been made prefect, Head Boy and
Captain of the rowing team. Whatever the top role is, Boris
wants it, whether it suits his abilities or not.

In lessons, Boris has impressed with his ready wit and
distinctive capacity with words. However, there are, it
pains me to say, some causes for concern. While Boris tends
to do well in unseens, tasks requiring research and
preparation are of markedly worse quality. He demonstrates
a somewhat cavalier attitude towards facts and veracity,
preferring to make colourful, sweeping statements and
reductive witticisms. When pressed on the accuracy (or
otherwise) of his claims, he will often respond with
mugging, gurning and what might uncharitably be described
as piffle-paffle.

As to discipline, Boris has troubled the Deputy Head less
frequently than some boys, but more frequently than others.
We note with regret the incident of provost and the whoopee
cushion, and hope the punishment he received has diminished
the appeal of such behaviour.

Perhaps my tone in the foregoing seems overly severe; if
so, I apologise. But having seen many a student pass
through these halls, I am keenly aware of how bad habits
can develop. Boris is self-evidently a remarkable boy.
Whether those remarks shall be positive or vituperative is
up to him.

Yours ever,

James Parham

James Parham

2

LENT

CHAPTER FOUR

Infinitus est numerus stultorum

Monday, 9th January

Greetings, dear Diary, and a Happy New Year! As you no doubt noticed, I chose not to update you during the time I was confined to the Johnson hovel. Needless to say, the whole business was brain-explodingly tedious. However, I am now back in my room at Eton, with the gorgeous Lady Farrah watching over me, so we shall resume our correspondence. Admittedly, that correspondence is a bit one-sided, but hey ho. Here are my New Year's resolutions:

- Each day, add at least two amusing words to my arsenal. Words like 'whangee' and 'furfuraceous'.
- Check pubic hair less frequently.
- Cement status as Eton's brightest young thing.

- Rack up a few more casualties in rugby.
- Otherwise, just keep on doing what I'm doing.

Had an excellent opportunity to fulfil no. 3 soon after getting dropped off. Passing through the common room, I spotted a poster advertising auditions for the school play. Mr Fotherington-Thomas, an English teacher and Europe's top-seeded weed, shall be directing a production of Shakespeare's *Richard III*. Having been starved of attention for the past few weeks, this struck me as manna from heaven, and I resolved to audition (naturally, I wish to play the king).

I lost no time in marching to the school library and checking out a copy of the play. Spent the afternoon marching around the courtyard, declaiming lines at great volume. Not the famous ones, about discontented winters, etc. – I just picked lines at random and belted them out with gusto. 'Upon what cause?' I cried, and 'My lord of Ely!' Some boys stopped and stared, but none approached; no doubt they were wary of disrupting my artistic process.

Perhaps it is as an actor that I shall secure my Great Manhood. I'm certainly good at pretending, and saying untrue things with conviction. Plus, there's my natural magnetism. People can't take their eyes off me (I know I can't, whenever there's a reflective surface about). A future as a screen idol would make a lot of sense. I can picture the marquees now: *Boris Johnson is James Bond 007 in You Only Die with a Golden Diamond Twice.*

Thursday, 12th January

My life as a thespian is off to roaring start. And to think I was actually worried this morning! Approaching the audition room, it felt as though a consignment of live butterflies had been dumped in my stomach. Fortunately, there's a limit to how nervous one can be when faced with a pushover like Mr Fotherington-Thomas. I entered to find the man shaking like a particularly excited leaf.

'Johnson!' he yelped. 'Glad you came in. Forgive me if I seem a little agitated: I'm just thrilled to be bringing the Great Bard's work to life.'

Of course he was. Mr F-T is what is known as a 'bardolator' or, as you or I would say, someone who's just plain nuts for Shakespeare. His classroom is chock-full of Shakespeare paraphernalia: pages from the First Folio, diagrams of the Globe and a big bronze bust of the man himself. I wouldn't be surprised to learn that he has a poster above his bed:

Willy S. on the beach, striking beefcake poses. He probably kisses it every night. You get the picture.

Anyway, I knew exactly how to play things as I began my audition.

'Before we get started,' I said, 'might I share something a bit personal?'

'Please do,' Fotherington-Thomas replied. 'I always encourage boys to express themselves, and acting is, after all, about truthfulness.'

'Well, I just wanted to say how much the works of William Shakespeare mean to me. From *Titus Andronicus* to *Timon of Athens*, my life has been infinitely enhanced by the immortal Bard.'

This brought a tear to the namby-pamby's eye, and so I continued:

'Yes, that great scion of Stratford means more to me than words can express. My heart beats to the rhythm of his iambic pentameter.'

Blah-blah-blah. Or, to put it in Shakespearean terms, blah-BLAH blah-BLAH blah-BLAH blah-BLAH blah-BLAH. Being a drip and a weed, Mr Fotherington-Thomas fell for this hook, line and sinker. Even before I delivered my monologue, I felt reasonably sure the part was mine.

74

Sure enough, I was offered the role of King Dick on the spot.

There are one or two flies in the ointment, though. First of all, Jessop-Jenkins has been cast as Richmond, painfully extending the amount of time I shall have to spend with him. Secondly, and more importantly, there's the issue of Richard. Having secured the role, I decided to spend my free time this evening actually reading the play. In so doing, I was troubled to find some of the language used to describe him: 'dreadful minister of hell', 'lump of foul deformity', 'abortive, rooting hog', etc. This seems a massive screw-up on Shakespeare's part. King Richard III – who, remember, is *the hero of the play* – is depicted as a twisted and malevolent hunchback. I suppose we'll have to make a few tweaks to the script. While I doubtless have considerable range as an actor, I can't imagine myself playing someone who isn't super popular and attractive.

Some call Master BoJo a liar,
A judgement both baseless and dire:
When he puts on an act,
Or fudges a fact,
He's telling a truth that is higher.

Sunday, 15th January

Had another run-in with that weirdo Rees-Mogg, when he passed me in the corridor.

'Oh dear,' he drawled, a single eyebrow raised. *'Errare humanum est . . .'*

I demanded to know what his problem was.

'Your shoes,' he replied. 'They are cross-laced, when of course they should be straight-laced.'

I scowled.

'They seem fine to me.'

'No doubt they do. But a true gentleman of Eton would be aware that we have worn our Oxfords straight-laced since George V, paying a visit to the school in the summer of 1912, was heard to express his preference for the style.'

When I asked whether he wanted to fix my laces himself, Rees-Mogg merely smirked and moved on. What an anachronistic buffoon! And not in a good way, like I am.

Ah well, onwards and upwards – rehearsals for *Richard III* start tomorrow. Spent all evening in my room, striking regal poses.

Monday, 16th January

Huge news, dear Diary: I, Alexander Boris de Pfeffel Johnson, am in love! Her name is Rubella St George (though, in due course, it will be 'Rubella Johnson'). As tempting as it is to fill the rest of your pages with nothing but that beauteous name, I shall attempt to describe our meeting.

I arrived at our first rehearsal with the fashionable lateness befitting a star. As expected, Mr Fotherington-Thomas was merely grateful that I had turned up at all.

'Good to see you, Boris!' he trilled. 'Now, as I was saying, in the time of Shakespeare, all female characters would be played by boys.'

My eyebrows shot up. I knew that Richard indulges in a spot of seduction, and I wasn't about to pitch woo at e.g. Bullard.

'Fortunately,' Mr F-T continued, 'we live in more enlightened times. With this in mind, I have asked students from Wycombe Abbey to portray the women of *Richard III.*'

A crackle of excitement ran through the assembled boys. The opportunity to interact with girls from nearby schools was the main reason anyone did an extracurricular. I myself stifled a yawn. Women assuredly had their uses – procreation, home maintenance, etc. – but these things were of no interest to me. At best, women were a pleasant frivolity, at worst a distraction from one's goals. Fotherington-Thomas quavered on:

'Our female colleagues should be arriving any moment now . . . Oh, and here they are!'

That's when I saw her. As the delegation from Wycombe Abbey shuffled inside, my eye was drawn to one figure, and one figure only. Oh, those platinum curls! Oh, those eyes of glacial blue! I had never felt this way about a girl before, and I swore, then and there, that I would stop at nothing to win her over.

The next thing I knew, Fotherington-Thomas had a hand on my shoulder and was leading me towards this earthbound goddess.

'Boris,' he said, 'you should get to know Rubella. She'll be playing Lady Anne, which means you have to court her.'

Well, for the first time I can recall, I was lost for words. Mr F-T skedaddled, leaving us face-to-face. Having mopped up most of my drool, I decided I should engage the lass in conversation.

'Hullo,' I gulped. 'My name's Al— Boris . . .'

I winced at the mistake. My lady shot me a smirk.

'Alboris? That's unusual.'

'No, it . . . it's Boris.'

'That's more common, but only just. So, Boris, what's this wretched play about? I only signed up for acting so I could get away from the Wycombe bitches.'

'Oh,' I said, 'well, I play the lead, Richard III, except, at the start of the play, I'm just Gloucester. Then I decide I'm going to do whatever it takes to become king.'

Watching the object of my desire stifle a yawn, I realised it would be wise to relate things back to her.

'Which is where you come in. Richard resolves to woo Anne Neville, the widow of Henry VI.'

'And how does he do that?'

'Well, he intercepts her late husband's funeral procession and attempts to seduce her over the corpse.'

'Oh dear,' said Rubella, wrinkling her inestimable nose, 'that sounds positively gruesome. Your Richard seems like a nasty little sod.'

Unable to think of a counterargument, I smiled weakly.

Towards the end of rehearsal, I took Fotherington-Thomas to one side.

'Sir,' I said, 'I appreciate more than most your faithful approach to the text. That said, I wonder if Richard could be portrayed in a slightly more sympathetic light.'

'But Boris,' Mr F-T protested, 'Richard is the embodiment of wickedness, akin to the character of Vice in medieval morality plays.'

'No, absolutely. On the other hand, wouldn't it be interesting if Richard was a six-pack-toting hunkorama, and Lady Anne wanted to get with him from the start?'

'I'm sorry, Boris,' the wimp replied, 'I don't think that reflects Shakespeare's intentions.'

Boo to Shakespeare! The thoughts of some ruff-wearing yokel are neither here nor there. How am I meant to win Rubella's heart if I'm playing a beastly hunchback?

MRS RUBELLa JOHNSON
—X—

Tuesday, 17th January

I have been tortured all day by thoughts of Rubella. How do I love her, dear Diary? Let me count the ways. First off, she is extremely pretty. She has a girlish little giggle that stirs the embers of my heart. She radiates pulchritude of the purest kind. And did I mention she's pretty? If my Eton contemporaries were to see such a filly on my arm, they would doubtless be impressed by my rugged machismo and proven heterosexuality.

Okay, reading that back, I'll concede that maybe I don't know all that much about Rubella's personality. In fact, I haven't the first clue what she's like. But does that matter? Love's not a game of *Trivial Pursuit*. Plus, I shall have time to discover her shoe size, her favourite colour, or any opinions she might have in future. For now, the important thing is that I'm a hundred per cent definitely in love. Goodnight, sweet Rubella. I am sure that you will be dreaming of me, just as I dream of you.

Monday, 23rd January

Late for rehearsals again, this time because I spent so long in front of the mirror, primping and preening for Rubella. Mr Fotherington-Thomas responded with his usual invertebracy:

'If you could try to get here a little more promptly in future, that would be amazing. It's just there aren't many scenes we can rehearse without Richard . . .'

More troubling are the censorious looks I'm starting to receive from my castmates. Then again: screw 'em. The only person whose feelings matter to me is my beloved Rubella. Alas, our interactions today were stilted, airless, devoid of rapport. At first I attributed it to my nerves, but increasingly I suspect it may be something deeper. We're clearly meant to be together, so why don't we enjoy each other's company?

At dinner, I chose to share these concerns with my intimate circle.

'Don't worry, Boris,' said Jessop-Jenkins. 'Girls are hard to understand. You've got to get to know them, is all.'

Edge-Llewelyn snorted at this.

'What the hell would you know about girls, Dom? You've got the word "virgin" running through you like a stick of rock.'

'That's not true!' Jessop-Jenkins erupted. 'I met a girl on holiday in Cornwall—'

'Oh yes? Was she riding a unicorn?'

After ten minutes of mocking Dominic, the conversation returned to my romantic travails.

'Before you start flirting, you need to know what you're working towards,' Ridgeley-Watts advised. 'By which I mean shagging.'

'Oh,' I replied, 'I know all about that. I've done it more times than I can count. But assuming I hadn't . . . how would I go about learning the, y'know . . . form?'

'Best thing you can do,' said Edge-Llewelyn, 'is get hold of a porn mag. I learned everything I know from *Fiesta*.'

Ridgeley-Watts concurred with this assessment, saying he had heard of a guy in sixth form who sells such magazines. It was suggested that the four of us all chip in on one, which could then be passed around for our private edification. My three companions agreed that this was a marvellous idea, and that I was the one who ought to make the exchange.

'The guy's name is Ford,' said Ridgeley-Watts, 'though everyone calls him the Pornbroker.'

I began to express reservations regarding the plan. After

all, Eton strictly prohibit licentious material on school grounds.

'What's the matter, Boz?' goaded Edge-Llewelyn. 'Aren't you a fan of naked women?'

My manhood thus challenged, I caved and agreed to buy the mag. The rest of dinner was spent deciding what kind of pornography we were in the market for. After some fierce debate, 'large breasts' emerged as a compromise candidate (though Ridgeley-Watts made a spirited argument for a genre called 'S&M').

Tuesday, 24th January

Via Ridgeley-Watts, I knew that Ford, aka the Pornbroker, has Geography first thing on a Tuesday, so this morning I intercepted him on his way there. While only sixteen years of age, Ford's sallow complexion and sunken eyes make him seem much older. As such, it was with some trepidation that I called out the following:

'Um, excuse me, are you Ford?'

He turned and regarded me with weary insolence.

'What do you want?'

I stepped towards him and lowered my voice to a whisper.

'My, erm, associates tell me that you may, uh, be able to facilitate certain . . . transactions . . .'

A long pause followed, as he scanned my features for sincerity. This guy was a professional, and didn't want to take any chances. For all he knew, I might be an informant, mounting a sting operation on behalf of the beaks. Finally, Ford spoke:

'What sort of thing you after?'

'Um . . .' I said, 'I was wondering . . . well . . . if you might have a – a periodical that focuses on, uh, large breasts . . .'

The man smirked at my tomato-faced embarrassment.

'I can get you a copy of *Busty Babes*,' he replied. 'Three quid. Meet me behind the dining hall at sundown. Make sure you're not followed.'

With that, he was gone. I knew my associates would balk at the princely sum of three quid, but was equally sure they would submit to the promise of *Busty Babes*.

This evening, as the sun dipped beneath the horizon, I arrived to make the trade. After ten minutes of skulking behind the dining hall, Ford appeared, wearing dark shades and a beaten-up leather coat. I handed him three pound coins, and he handed me the magazine, concealed inside a copy of the *Daily Telegraph*.

'Enjoy, kid. If you get caught, you never heard of me.'

He stepped backwards, melting into the shadows. As smut-pedlars go, I must say this Ford is impressive.

Managed to ferry the precious cargo back to my room without incident. I had nightmarish visions of Old Crighty sneaking up on me and demanding to borrow my *Telegraph* for its cryptic crossword. He would then open the broadsheet and be confronted with the very un-cryptic front cover of *Busty Babes*. Fortunately, no such thing transpired. I spread the magazine out on my bed, and was about to, shall we say, get to grips with it, when Edge-Llewelyn burst in and grabbed the thing.

'Sorry, Boz,' he said, 'but getting the mag was my idea, so I should have the first night with it.' He swept out again, taking with him the myriad babes. Given this was all supposedly a means of educating me, I felt somewhat hard done by. Also, just hard.

MY HEROES
by
Boris Johnson

PART TWO

WINSTON CHURCHILL

Our national hero, Churchill single-handedly won World War Two despite being an obese alcoholic. He did this by making splendid speeches on the wireless, in which he would repeat himself until Johnny Commoner was nice and inspired. This led to German surrender and the Führer topping himself (there was also some business involving the Yanks and Stalingrad, but it was mainly the speeches).

Some wets like to point out that Winston advocated the use of poisoned gas against 'uncivilised tribes' and was responsible for a famine that killed four million Bengalis. But what these Trotskyists forget is that Churchill defeated the Nazis, even though he believed in a lot of the same stuff they did. Basically, he wasn't as bad as Hitler, which is why he's the greatest Englishman who ever lived.

I myself would like nothing more than to follow in old Winnie's footsteps (especially if it means I can flick the Vs at people without getting told off).

Saturday, 28th January

Ventured into Windsor to take in a showing of this new science fiction film everyone's raving about. My expectations weren't high for *Star Wars*, but I actually found it rather thrilling. It's a jolly space romp, featuring mystic warrior-monks, planets getting blown up and a homosexual robot. Some of my classmates have suggested that, with my blue eyes and helmet of blond hair, I resemble the film's hero, Luke Skywalker. I couldn't disagree more – Luke is a wimp, mewling to his uncle about picking up power converters, etc. I'm much more like Han Solo: the sly, raffish bad boy, who shoots first and asks questions later. Which I suppose would make Jessop-Jenkins a sort of weedy Chewbacca.

CHAPTER FIVE

Acta est fabula, plaudite!

Wednesday, 1st February

Received a fair amount of opprobrium from my castmates for being tardy to rehearsal. Honestly, if it bothers them so much, why don't they simply turn up half an hour late themselves? The other charge being levelled at me is that, several weeks in, I remain resolutely off book. Well, forgive me if memorising lines isn't my main priority. Honestly, I have no idea what they're worried about – there's plenty of time before opening night, and I'm a notoriously fast learner. But try telling that to the moaning minnies who play Clarence, Brackenbury et al.

Think I might be starting to make headway with Rubella. Exhibiting the same boldness I did in acquiring *Busty Babes*, I have made a point of chatting to her at every possible juncture. If another boy engages her in conversation, I instantly shut it down. Good techniques are to give the guy a dead arm when she's not looking, or to approach them, loudly saying: 'Ah, X, did you ever get hold of that haemorrhoid cream?'

In truth, my darling R isn't the easiest nut to crack, conversationally. Her primary interests are hockey, horses and horticulture. Still, my quips are increasingly greeted with smirks and giggles, so I am confident she will come around. After all, what warm-blooded woman could withstand the Johnson brio?

Wednesday, 8th February

Once again, the authorities have come down like a tonne of bricks on Bad Boy Boris. At the moment, I can't go two days without getting written up for something, whether it's being tardy or else disruptive in class. Most often, I am accused of 'fecklessness', which sounds like an Irish term for virginity. Today I was given georgics, a punishment wherein one is made to copy hundreds of lines from the Virgil snooze-a-thon of the same name. Naturally, this serves as a mental torture, before one even factors in the carpal tunnel-wrecking agony of the enterprise.

Virgil's aren't the only lines causing me grief. This afternoon, the *Richard III* crew had a conniption over me flubbing a bit of dialogue. 'Boris,' they mewled as one, 'the play is next week and you're still not off book!' How many times do I have to tell these people? I have an exceptional memory, and could probably memorise the entire text over breakfast. Those lines shall be learned in due course. Alas, I must now end this entry, as my hand is cramping like the blazes.

Thursday, 9th February

Following a somewhat ropey rehearsal, Mr Fotherington-Thomas asked me to stay behind.

'Now Boris,' he said, 'I'm going to speak to you man to man. This play is important to me, and not just because it's by the great Bard of Stratford-upon-Avon. Like you, I only started at Eton a few months ago. This production is my first chance to show the Headmaster that he made the right choice in hiring me. So, will you promise you'll learn your lines?'

'Of course,' I replied. 'I swear on all that is holy. In fact, I shall be practising this very evening.'

Spent an enjoyable evening throwing rocks at pigeons.

Friday, 10th February

Bit of a dispute in rehearsal today. We were due to practise Act V, Scene 5, which kicks off as follows:

'Alarum. Enter King Richard and Richmond; they fight; Richard is slain.'

Alaruming indeed. As you'll recall, the part of Richmond is being played by my underling, Dominic Jessop-Jenkins. No doubt you can anticipate my complaint. As we were about to start blocking the death scene, I raised my hand.

'Yes, Boris?' said Mr Fotherington-Thomas.

'So, in this scene, Richard is killed in single combat with Richmond, later Henry VII?'

'Correct.'

'And how attached are we to that?'

'Pardon?'

I adopted my most reasonable tone.

'I just think it strains credulity that I could be defeated by a weed like Jessop-Jenkins. No offence, Dom.'

'Oh, I don't mind,' said Jessop-Jenkins, though not as emphatically as I might have liked.

'I'm not sure what you're saying,' moaned Mr F-T. 'Are you suggesting we replace Jessop-Jenkins?'

'No! No, no, no. I'm suggesting that I kill Jessop-Jenkins, instead of the other way round. I mean, wouldn't it be a better ending if Richard won and kept on being king?'

Fotherington-Thomas visibly strained to suppress some kind of outburst.

'Well,' he said, 'clearly Shakespeare didn't feel that way.'

'True,' I conceded, 'but must we be so bound by convention? Is not every performance an act of reinterpretation?'

'Richard was killed in the Battle of Bosworth Field. That is a matter of historical record.'

'Is it though? I'm sure some sources bear you out on that. Others might disagree.'

'Now really, Boris,' said Mr Fotherington-Thomas, with a level of exasperation unusual for him, 'I have done my best to accommodate you at every turn. But this is a bridge too far.'

Clearly, the bloke's love of the Bard had put some steel in his spine. All around me, cast members muttered darkly.

'. . . not a team player . . .'

'. . . just one thing after another . . .'

'. . . doesn't even know his bloody lines . . .'

Strewth! I suppose I should have expected this when I went into acting – the profession is full of divas.

Saturday, 11th February

Today Edge-Llewelyn outdid himself by hosting a midnight feast. It seems his uncle had visited Windsor, bringing with him a hamper of delicacies. The scrumptious items upon which we gorged came from all over Europe: French foie gras, Spanish olives, Italian prosciutto, Dutch gouda and, for dessert, Austrian *Vanillekipferl* and the delicious Gundel pancakes of Hungary.

God, I love the Continent! To think there are those in this country who would sever ties with our European cousins! Certainly, I could never support any policy that might endanger such enriching cultural exchange.

In Britain, our fine public schools
Instil a firm sense of the rules:
For there we are taught
To never get caught,
As punishment's only for fools.

Tuesday, 14th February

I am writing this on what was, without hyperbole, the worst day of my life. And to think everything was going so well, until . . . Well, we'll get to that.

I awoke feeling somewhat apprehensive. Truth be told, I had perhaps displayed a rather blasé approach to line-learning. But this was nothing that couldn't be rectified. Putting my acting skills to use, I feigned tuberculosis, getting out of the day's lessons and giving myself time to go over the text. There's a marvellous Greek word for memories like mine: eidetic, which means one can bring images to mind with perfect clarity. I was confident that, after a couple of hours, I would know my lines like the back of my thingummy.

As such, I rewarded myself with an afternoon of Curly Wurlies and lazing, then set off to do the show as calm as you like. I arrived at the theatre, barely late at all, and joined my castmates for the verbal warm-up (stuff like 'you know New York, you need New York, you know you need unique New York' and 'the lips, the teeth, the tip of the tongue'). Mr Fotherington-Thomas gave us what he doubtless thought

97

an inspiring speech, and soon I was outfitted in my robe, tunic and prosthetic hump. As I waited for the curtain to rise, I glanced at the opposite wing, where ravishing Rubella stood, all dolled up as Lady Anne. Soon the curtain rose and a fanfare played. I stepped into the limelight and boomed in my clearest, most actorly voice:

> *Now is the winter of our discontent*
> *Made glorious summer by this sun of York;*
> *And all the clouds . . . Oh, crikey . . .*

I realised then that I had no idea what the next line was. Everything I thought I knew had deserted me, as my memory proved less eidetic than pathetic. I stared into space, alarmed and ashamed, conscious that the entire school was watching. Had I, Boris Johnson, finally fallen victim to hubris? Then I realised what I needed to do: in the words of Donald O'Connor in *Singin' in the Rain*, I had to make 'em laugh. I snapped back to reality.

'Ah yes, right, clouds. What are these clouds up to, then? Hopefully not raining on anyone's parade. Maybe they have a silver lining. As I understand it, that's standard operating procedure for clouds.'

I pulled a face, and laughter rippled from the audience, as welcome as rain on the Sahara. Heartened, I continued:

'Bosom! Yes, that's it – the clouds are doing something related to bosoms. In fact, they're buried in the deep bosom of the ocean. Lucky old clouds! I imagine quite a few of us wouldn't mind being buried in a bosom.'

A resounding laugh. I glanced at the wings, where Mr Fotherington-Thomas stood, his features frozen in a horrified rictus. Ah well, I thought, no turning back: *Richard III* was now a comedy.

The guffaws just kept on coming. Other cast-members would enter to wanly deliver their lines, as I mugged and riffed and improvised around them. At some points I would loudly call to Fotherington-Thomas for prompts; at others, I would dash into the wings, then emerge with a copy of Shakespeare's *Complete Works*. By the time we got to Act V, Scene 4, people were rolling in the aisles. Having cried 'A horse! A horse! My kingdom for a horse!', I leapt offstage and began asking audience members, one by one, if they knew where I could find such a beast.

When the curtain call came, I received a thunderous standing ovation, which I accepted by bowing, then throwing my crown into the audience. Despite this euphoric reception, the atmosphere backstage was distinctly sour. Mr Fotherington-Thomas, as pale as a bed sheet, rocked back and forth on his heels, emitting a low hum. Jessop-Jenkins, of all people, avoided my gaze. In a particularly nasty scene, Dalrymple, who had played the Duke of Buckingham, stepped up and started jabbing his finger into my chest.

'We spent weeks rehearsing that play! You're a selfish prick, Boris Johnson!'

Mercifully, this moment was broken when Fotherington-Thomas fainted.

Given such unpleasantness, I was especially keen to get back to the auditorium and soak up some adulation. The boys of Eton were uniform in their praise. I was a comedic legend, funnier than Tommy Cooper, John Cleese, or the Two Ronnies combined. Even my old foe Piers Davenant remarked on how hilarious I was. I lapped this up for a while, then went in search of Rubella.

Now struck me as the perfect time to make a move: not only was I still on a high from my theatrical triumph, but it was Valentine's Day, for goodness' sake! I wasn't worried that she might hold my scene-stealing against me – she had made it clear that, on her list of concerns, this production ranked alongside Peruvian basket-weaving. I intercepted her outside the theatre.

'I say, Rubella!'

She turned, confronting me with her gelid loveliness.

'Oh,' she said. 'Hi.'

'Hullo,' I responded. 'Y'know, it was a pleasure, um, acting alongside you. I thought your Anne really was tremendous. And, now that we're no longer working together, it occured to me that, uh . . .'

She rolled her eyes.

'What do you want, Boris?'

It was now or never. Faint heart never won fair lady. *Audentes fortuna iuvat.*

'So, uh . . .' I said, more nervous than I'd ever felt onstage, 'I wondered whether you might, um, be interested in . . . filling the position . . . of being . . . my girlfriend.'

'No,' she said, without a pause, 'I don't think I'll be doing that.'

'What?' I exclaimed. 'But . . . but why?'

'Why would I?' she replied. 'Firstly, I'm thirteen – I'm not on the lookout for a boyfriend. Secondly, you and I have zero rapport, and nothing in common.'

I sputtered, my mind reeling.

'I–I . . . But that's absurd! Give me one good reason why we shouldn't be an item!'

'You want me to be honest?'

'Naturally.'

'Well, Boris, I don't like you. All you can talk about is yourself, and, whenever anyone else talks, you tune out and start planning your next quip. You obviously think of yourself as a charmer, but then treat everyone around you like crap – especially that Jenkins-Jessop guy. You're arrogant, deluded and a compulsive liar. And I think a lot of that comes down to you not liking yourself.'

With that, she departed, leaving me to sweep up the pieces of my shattered heart. Who would have thought a Shakespeare play could end in tragedy?

THE BOZFATHER

A screenplay by Boris Johnson

EXT. ETON COLLEGE – DAY

We open on the mean streets of Eton. Through them strides a big, tough Italian, DON BORISONI. Unusually, he's blond, but he wears very shiny suits and everyone's afraid of him. Borisoni is approached by DOMINO JESSOPONI-JENKINSO, a weed.

DOMINO

Don Borisoni, I am-a having trouble with-a de beak di matematica. He give-a me too much a-homework.

Borisoni waves his hand.

BORISONI

Guh wuh blurgle murgle gugh ugh bluh.

(At this point, I should mention that Don Borisoni keeps a bunch of marbles in his mouth, so it's nigh on impossible to make out what he's saying. Jessoponi-Jenkinso seems happy, though).

DOMINO

Grazie, signore!

The cove dashes off, leaving Borisoni to go into a trattoria and dig into a bloody great bowl of spaghetti, with lashings of red wine.

BORISONI

Glurble blurb.

(Translation: *molto bene*, i.e. very good).

Just then, one of Borisoni's goons, with slicked-back hair and a scar over one eye, comes hurtling into the restaurant.

RIDGELEY-WATTSO

Don Borisoni! I'm afraid the heads of the other families are plotting against you: Don Camerozzi, Don Davenanza, even the *capo di tutti capi*, Don Crighto.

Don Borisoni is so alarmed that he spits out his marbles.

BORISONI

Ooh, gosh, crikey!

CUT TO:

INT. DINING ROOM – NIGHT

The heads of the rival families (including Dons Camerozzi, Davenanza and Crighto) sit around a table, with Don Borisoni at the head.

DON BORISONI
(Sans marbles)

Gentlemen, I hope you enjoyed your pasta. For dessert, I thought you might like some hot lead.

[Jessoponi-Jenkinso and Ridgeley-Wattso burst in, holding tommy guns.]

DONS CAMEROZZI, DAVENANZA AND CRIGHTO
Oh-a no-a!

They all get riddled with bullets, then slump face down into their pasta sauce. Don Borisoni has won, and he didn't even have to try that hard.

IL END-O.

Stirring stuff, eh? As I see it, the main thing to nail down is who should play Don Borisoni. Robert Redford? John Travolta? Burt Reynolds? I worry none of them are handsome enough.

CHAPTER SIX

Mundus vult decipi, ergo decipiatur

Tuesday, 21st February

A week has passed, but done nothing to numb the pain. Jessop-Jenkins tries to comfort me by bringing cups of hot chocolate and abundant toast. I tell him there's no point, but that he should keep doing it. I may not be an expert in heartbreak, but I know that what I'm feeling now is worse than anything anyone else has ever felt.

Ugh, why am I so weedy? You wouldn't catch Pericles blubbing over some bird, or Genghis Khan staggering round the Mongol plains, crying 'Woe is me!' I used to think I was similarly tough, yet here I am, laid low by a tootsie.

Wednesday, 22nd February

Just when I think things can't get any worse, I receive a letter from Rachel:

Dear King Boris,

So it would seem that my big bro is now too much of a prodigy to respond to my letters. Well, I shall not let this deter me, for I dread to think what mishaps would befall you without my advice and tutelage. Peshaps you might jump inside an abandoned well, or trade all your earthly possessions for some magic beans. In any case, I will continue to write, no matter how thankless the task.

yours offendedly

Rachel

P.S. I am turning Bestie against you, and if you don't reply soon, I shall train him to attack you on sight.

Saturday, 25th February

In an attempt to lift me from my rut, Dominic, Edge-Llewelyn and Ridgeley-Watts decided we should venture into London for a day out. Predictably, this was a complete disaster. First off, it rained torrentially from the moment our train drew into Charing Cross. Secondly, despite us wearing our most inconspicuous attire (Harris tweed jackets, baggy corduroys and sweaters), we were harassed by oiks throughout. Having bought some dodgy kebabs on Old Compton Street, to consume which we had to fend off a horde of pigeons, we wandered damply to St James's Park. It was there that things went from bad to abominable.

As we skulked towards Buckingham Palace, I spotted a young couple heading in our direction, hand in hand. It was with a chill akin to liquid nitrogen that I recognised the girl: Rubella St George. Still worse: the chap holding her hand was none other than DAVID CAMERON. Oh, that it should come to this; that I should have to see my love cavort with my greatest enemy! Frailty, thy name is woman!

Aware of my discomfort, Jessop-Jenkins proposed that we go and look at the ducks. But it was too late: the happy couple had seen us.

'All right, chaps?' exclaimed Cameron. 'Rubella and I thought we'd go for a romantic stroll. Shame about the weather!'

I stared at the ground in an effort to maintain my composure. Perhaps noticing this, Cameron blustered on.

'I suppose I should thank you, old chap. Ru and I met after that little play you were in, and now we're an item.'

'Hello, Boris,' said Rubella.

'Good to see you,' I murmured, though this was directed more towards my shoes than her.

'Hang on,' said Cameron, 'didn't *you* try and ask her out? Can't say I blame you, old chap: Rubella's quite a catch.'

At this point, something within me snapped. Suddenly, all my heartbreak came burbling forth.

'How could you betray me like this?' I howled at Rubella. She met this with a look of astonishment.

'Steady on, pal!' Cameron cried.

Rubella said: 'Betray? I don't know what you're talking about.'

'To think I loved you!' I squawked, then ran off towards Trafalgar Square. I rounded a corner, then was violently sick. In retrospect, it's hard to tell how much of that was the emotional distress, and how much was the kebab.

Sunday, 26th February

Last night, a concerned Mr Parham swung by my room. He observed that something seemed to have taken the wind out of my sails, and asked if there was anything he could do to help. I briefly considered asking if he would help me drop Dave Cameron in the Thames with a pair of cement shoes, but chose not to. Parham – who I suppose isn't such a bad sort – then suggested I was in need of stimulation, and that I should perhaps find a new extracurricular activity.

'We know from the *Richard* fiasco that you're not exactly a team player, so maybe something a bit more solitary. Have you considered getting involved with the *Eton College Chronicle*?'

Of course, I dismissed this at first, as I do any suggestion, but, the more I thought about it, the more clearly I could see myself as a newspaperman.

I awoke this morning, raring to write an article. And I knew just what the subject should be. Cracking open my notepad, I set down the title 'Girls: an Exposé'. Words began to flow out of me:

Eve. Lilith. Catherine de Medici. What do these individuals have in common? All of them are girls. Throughout history, girls have been a scourge upon society. Whatever idiot designated them the 'fairer sex' was clearly off his rocker – women are, by their very nature, unfair. They strut about, releasing oestrogen and other hormones, in an effort to brainwash men and make us soppy. Then, when we act upon this soppiness by asking them to go steady, they mock and reject us. We public school boys must therefore cherish these years of seclusion, before we are compelled to acquire girlfriends, wives and mistresses.

I spun this theme into a tight 1,000 words, then stomped off to find the *Chronicle*'s editor, one Charles Corkingham-Blount. He read my piece with roars of appreciative laughter, then offered me a regular opinion column, which I gratefully accepted. Perhaps this is how I will become a Great Man: in that most honourable of professions, journalism.

Monday, 27th February

For the past forty-eight hours, I have been simply teeming with column ideas. Any time a subject is raised, lo and behold: I have an opinion on it. Whether it's trades unions, X-rated films or the Arab-Israeli conflict, your man Boris will take to his typewriter and hammer out the expected word count. It's so obvious to me now that this is my *raison d'être*: I shall fill the world with my voice and my views. And if people don't like those views? I can always get new ones.

WHY WE SHOULD RELAX SCHOOL UNIFORM
By Boris Johnson

Once in a blue moon, it falls to the younger generation to step up and right a wrong that has persisted throughout history. From the Suffragettes of the 1900s, to the American Civil Rights Movement, brave souls have time and again been called upon to address injustice. Today, my fellow Etonians, that call goes out to us. The injustice? Our school's archaic and cruel school uniform policy.

The masters will not thank me for this intervention, but it is a deeply personal subject, on which I have held strong views for years. As classical scholars will know, the word 'uniform' derives from the Latin uni, meaning 'one', and form, meaning 'form'. We are a school of some one thousand two hundred boys — tell me, is there any one form of clothing that could meet all our diverse needs? If such fabled vestments exist, they are surely not the ludicrous penguin suits and larynx-crushing bowties that Eton currently requires.

No doubt fans of so-called "Political Correctness" are keen on the current situation. They are the opponents of individualism, and would hate to see the average Etonian sport his groovy threads. Instead, they would relegate us to the drab sameness of tailsuit, waistcoat and bowtie. Such enforced conformity would not be out of place in the China of Mao Zedong, or Stalin's Russia. You know who else liked uniforms?

That's right: the Nazis. Whose boss, if you recall, was HITLER.

So please, comrades: join me in rejecting the strictures of the sadistic school elite. For too long the masters have treated us as pinstriped prisoners, imposing upon us a dreary uniform designed to strip one of one's style, one's character, one's very personhood. In addition, our pretentious costume invites the oikish inhabitants of Windsor to victimise us by hurling cruel words and even crueller bottles. The only adequate response to this is a full sartorial revolution.

Students of Eton unite: you have nothing to lose but your ties!

ETON COLLEGE
CHRONICLE

WHY WE SHOULDN'T RELAX SCHOOL UNIFORM
By Boris Johnson

I have no desire to stoke division by wading into so contentious an area, but this is a deeply personal subject, on which I have held strong views for years. Like all sensible people, sound in both body and mind, I ardently oppose any meddling with our fine school uniform. I find it frankly staggering that anyone could have the arrogance, the impertinence, and the sheer moist-brained stupidity to argue otherwise.

The claim is that these sumptuary laws are inhibiting to boys' creativity and self-expression. To that I say tish, biddlewhack and gumph. We are gentlemen and scholars, not It Girls tottering round Carnaby Street in high-heel boots! If anything, wearing the same gear brings out our personalities all the more. Plus, there will be ample opportunity to play dress up once we proceed to university (Oxford, or — if we mess up very badly — Cambridge).

No doubt fans of so-called "Political Correctness" are keen to tear the current system down — another harmless custom of the upper class abolished. But how would these spite-mongers have us dress, we future writers, academics and statesmen? Perhaps we could adopt the tie-dyed, patchouli-stinking garb of the hippy? The spiked, neon hair and metal-strewn visage of the punk? The sparkling accoutrements and flared trousers of the disco dancer? No, dear friends, we are Etonians, and should not be ashamed to wear the traditional outfit of our tribe. Mark that word: tradition. The boys of Eton have been wearing tailsuit, waistcoat and bowtie for centuries. When deranged Trotskyites argue that we should change our uniform, they are attempting to erase history. And it is precisely this rejection of traditional values that led to the brutal regimes of Stalin and Mao Zedong. Ask yourself: are you willing to risk the deaths of millions of people, just so that you may wear a T-shirt to Geography?

For the true patriot, there can be only one answer: if it ain't broke, don't fix it.

Monday, 6th March

Wrote rather a topping column about the '75 referendum, and how the UK did absolutely the right thing by joining the European community. 'If membership of the Common Market is good enough for the estimable Mrs Thatcher,' I said, 'then it is good enough for me. Ever since my boyhood in Belgium, I have been a fervent advocate of closer relations with Europe, and I cannot see myself changing my mind in future.' Pretty wise, if I say so myself.

Friday, 10th March

It occurs to me that I've rather left you out in the cold, dear Diary, I suppose my other biggest project has been getting revenge on David Cameron. This is easier said than done: unlike Timothy Fitznigel, our Dave is a canny operator, who seems almost immune to pranks. I sneak a laxative into his coffee, and suddenly he decides he's had enough. I leave drawing pins on his chair, and he swaps places with another boy. At first I thought he must be some kind of mastermind, always three steps ahead of me. However, I'm increasingly coming to think that he leads a charmed existence.

Anyway, I decided to put my anti-Cameron campaign on hold when I received the following letter:

Boris,

I really must insist you stop persecuting poor David. It is monstrously immature to pursue a vendetta against someone simply because they are involved with a girl you fancy. I suspect you're also jealous because, while you merely act like an aristocrat, Dave is the real thing. If, as you claim, you ever had true feelings for me, then I would ask that you leave us alone.

Yours platonically,

Rubella

You know what? To hell with them both! Perhaps fate isn't so sweet on Cameron after all, if it would condemn him to spending his days with that dreary prig, Rubella St George!

Sunday, 12th March

Was putting the finishing touches to this week's piece ('A Call for More Attractive Dames') when Charles C-B burst into my room in a state of high dudgeon.

'For goodness' sake, Boris,' he hissed, 'you've really done it now.'

It emerged that various members of staff were unhappy about my latest column, 'Why Beaks Are for the Birds'. To support my argument, I had confected a few choice quotes, such as Mr Crighton saying: 'My dream in life is to murder a boy and make it look like an accident.' Now Crighton et al. were bleating about libel. I felt sure that Charles was overreacting.

'What are they going to do, sue us?'

'No, but the school could withdraw our funding.'

A shiver ran down my spine. Clearly, the guy was serious.

'Look, we shouldn't get carried away here. I was just trying to entertain.'

'Everyone thinks you're entertaining,' said Corkingham-Blount. 'But these are serious ethical violations. Which I wouldn't care about, except you got caught. I'm afraid I'm going to have to let you go . . .'

I begged him to reconsider, alas, to no avail. So there we are. Not only am I *persona non grata* with the only woman I ever loved, but now I've been stripped of my column, the one thing that gave life meaning. I suppose I should be grateful for this lesson. If I should ever again find myself a journalist, I will be sure not to fabricate quotes, or just make stuff up wholesale.

THOUGHTS AND OBSERVATIONS PERTAINING TO THE NORTH OF ENGLAND, WHICH I HAVE NEVER HAD THE DISPLEASURE OF VISITING

An essay by Boris Johnson.

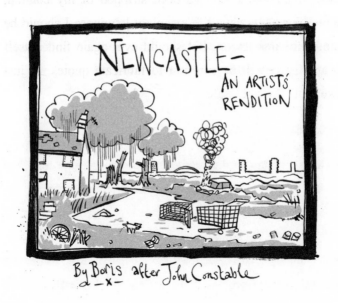

By Boris after John Constable
_—x—

While the existence of the English upper class is rightfully celebrated, it comes at a terrible price, which is to say the existence of the so-called 'working' class. We in the South generally manage to keep our commoners in line, but the same cannot be said of the North. Here, the lower orders comprise of twinkly-eyed porters, buxom chambermaids and toothless old cockneys who wish you 'good evenin', guv'nah!' There, alas, the Great Unwashed run rampant. As an Etonian, there is no reason why you should ever enter the North, except if you make a bish of Oxbridge admissions and end up at Durham.* However, if you get on the wrong train, or become Prime Minister and are forced to campaign in Leeds, here's what you should know.

Geography and Climate

The North of England is generally said to stretch from the Scottish border to the River Trent (although, as far as I'm concerned, everything above Stratford-upon-Avon can happily be written off). Its major cities are Manchester (hooliganism, drugs), Liverpool (self-pity, stolen hubcaps) and Newcastle (random violence, shirtlessness in December). Weather comes

---

* Fortunately, that ancient university is well-fortified against marauders from the surrounding region, and has a very high concentration of ex-public schoolboys. Think of it as an oasis in this desert of flat caps and people calling you 'man'.

in the form of constant rain, broken occasionally by hail-stones. The most common wildlife in the region are wolves, vultures and hyenas. Its chief export is despair.

Northerners and Their 'Culture'

By far the most dangerous thing about the North is North-erners. Northerners are between four and five feet tall, largely bipedal, and tend to have names like Shazza, Wazza, Kazza or Bazza. They possess an array of bizarre and impen-etrable accents, from the strangulated outrage of the Scouse, to the amiable slurring of the Geordie.

Denizens of this blasted realm fill their time in a variety of ways. The most popular leisure activity is coal mining, to the extent that most Northern males spend every sunlit hour underground, emerging only at night to get pissed. The Northern female can be found either at the tanning salon, or howling invective at her vast brood of children. While a Southern gentleman might amuse himself by taking in the cricket at Lord's, the Northern man does so by watching a bar fight.

A Note Regarding Scotland

While Scotland is not technically part of the North, it shares many of that region's characteristics. Much as smoking marijuana can serve as a precursor to harder drug use, Scots are what happens when you leave Northerners to their own devices. This is not to tar all of Scotland with the same brush: parts of Edinburgh are lovely, and I know some bloody good chaps with estates in the Highlands.

Summing Up

In conclusion, the North is a land of contrasts.* While I hope and pray that I never have to set foot in it, I must admit to a certain admiration for the hardy folk who manage to live there. As the stoic Geordie might slur, having downed his seventh pint of the morning: 'Why aye, man, yous are reet Bobby Dazzlers!'

---

* On the one hand, it's appalling; on the other, it's hideous.

Friday, 24th March

End of term meeting with Parham was less painful than expected. I imagine he's treating me with kid gloves, given my recent and extensive funk.

'There's always something whirring away in that head of yours,' he said. 'But I think you'd be a lot happier if you could apply your mental energy to something other than yourself.'

Tomorrow I return home for the holidays, and I shall do so a bruised, battered, beaten and bested Boris. Reading over these entries, I find myself asking: what did I do wrong? How did I go from cock of the walk to just a regular cock? Munching a desolate piece of toast before bedtime, I had this epiphany: every time I was thwarted, it was because I let down my defences. Because I was vulnerable, spontaneous or uncalculated. As myself, I'm just a scared schoolboy. But when I am one with my persona, I am unstoppable. The conclusion is obvious: I must come back next term devoid of human weaknesses. If I am to succeed in my aims, I need to be Boris 24/7.

ETON COLLEGE
SCHOOL REPORT

STUDENT NAME: Boris Johnson   **HALF:** Lent

I'm afraid I must provide a mixed report of Boris' conduct and achievements over the past few months. In some respects he would seem to be thriving: he is popular and well-liked, on course to become something of a college legend. At the same time, his academic efforts have become worryingly slapdash, and his behaviour is often intolerable. He appears more than willing to risk censure, and betray the trust of others, in order to increase his popularity among the boys. In the past fortnight alone, he is suspected of having spread rumours about Haddon-Peyton's private life, perpetrated lewd graffiti, and attached a fire-cracker to the tail of the college dog. Such antics have won him few friends among the teaching staff. Mr Fotherington-Thomas, in particular, has found his association with Boris deleterious, and has been forced to go and recuperate at his mother's house in St Leonards.

It has been heartening, this term, to see Boris so enthused by the possibilities of the written word. Alas, his tenure as columnist for the Eton College Chronicle serves as a vivid illustration that written words can be highly destructive. We teachers expect a certain degree of ribbing from the student body, but Boris' article "Mr Tuffield's Twelve-Hooker-a-Night Lifestyle" went far beyond the pale. His exposé of the Head Matron, who, he alleges, is the kingpin of an international drugs cartel, was similarly dismaying.

More troubling than any one infraction, though, is Boris' conviction that verbal cleverness absolves him of the need to tell the truth. As I have repeatedly attempted to impress upon him, the truth is not a game: it is our duty, and the foundation of any society worth living in. Without truth, I need hardly tell you, real human connection becomes impossible. I hope you are able to reinforce this message over the holidays, as I am truly fond of Boris, and would hate to see him go further down the path of mendacity.

Yours ever,

James Parham

James Parham

3

SUMMER

CHAPTER SEVEN

In flagrante delicto

Monday, 24th April

Returned to Eton after what felt like an eternity of domestic tedium. To my perturbation, though, something seems to have changed here. As I walk through the courtyard, I no longer provoke cries of 'Boris, legend!' Boys are no longer clamouring round me, eager to hear a wisecrack. At dinner, I saw David Cameron surrounded by a cluster of my fellows, who were chortling and hanging on his every word. Dear Diary, it was as much as I could do to force down my rat linguini.

I also note that Edge-Llewelyn and Ridgeley-Watts are treating me with, if not *froideur*, then certainly an odd level of reserve. Sure, Jessop-Jenkins still follows me around, puppy-like, but that's just a basic fact of existence. I mean, one isn't grateful for gravity . . .

There once was a chap, David Cam,
Whose face was the colour of ham.
Some thought him a star,
But Boris was far
More brilliant, so he had to scram!

Tuesday, 25th April

Was gallivanting down Windsor High Street when I spotted a group of hippy subversives. They were loitering about, smoking roll-up cigarettes and loudly discussing Palestine. To my chagrin, one of the Trots approached me: a heavily corduroyed figure, sporting floppy brown hair, a bushy beard and a Lenin cap.

'Hello there,' he said, smiling rodentially. 'Could you spare a minute or two?'

'Who the hell are you?' I replied, with more politeness than the situation merited.

'The name's Jeremy. Jeremy Corbyn.'

The chap stuck out a hand, but didn't seem too bothered when I declined to shake it. He continued:

'I'm a Labour councillor from north London. Me and

some mates are spending the day in Windsor, to investigate how the ruling class perpetuates its hold on power. Would you be willing to answer some questions on the obscene privilege that Eton embodies?'

I narrowed my eyes. This sounded far from ideal.

'Why exactly do you want to know about my school?'

The man continued to grin cluelessly.

'Well, so we can break its stranglehold on our nation's government, and thus transfer power to the workers.'

Now, I wouldn't describe myself as a political person, but when some beardy interloper takes aim at the venerable institution to which I belong, this is liable to put the Johnson back up.

'Why don't you naff off?' I exclaimed. Corbyn took it on the chin; clearly he was used to such reactions.

'Look, I'm not attacking you. You're just an innocent kid. It's not your fault all your friends and family are evil.'

I informed him that, if he didn't leave me alone, I would fetch College security and have him beaten in the street.

'Fair enough,' he said, his equanimity undimmed. 'If you ever find yourself in Harringay, drop by one of our discussion groups cum Peruvian weaving circles.'

With that, the filthy hippy turned on his heel and departed.

It took me a long shower and a brace of Curly Wurlies to recover from the encounter.

Wednesday, 26th April

Against all logic, today I found myself wondering about some of the things that the deranged Bolshevik Corbyn had said. Was I really the beneficiary of a rigged system, the complacent inheritor of obscene privilege? I soon shook off such ludicrous notions. Those who prosper under the capitalist system do so because of their hard work and moral probity. Also, maybe poor people *like* being poor – has the loony left considered that?

As for privilege, I've had to overcome tremendous obstacles to get where I am. I can't recall what they were right now, but they definitely exist.

MY HEROES
by

Boris Johnson

PART THREE

Maggie Thatcher is the Leader of the Opposition and, as far as I'm concerned, would be a damn sight better as PM than old Callaghan. Despite being female, she doesn't, by all accounts, spend her days gossiping, washing her hair or going hysterical. In fact, she doesn't seem to have any emotions whatsoever.

When she was Education Secretary, Maggie took milk away from the poor kids, which I think was a jolly good idea. Firstly, the country needed to rein in spending – we're not made of milk. Secondly, calcium encourages the development of strong bones, and the last thing we need is a bunch of super-powered oiks roaming about.

As boring as I find politics, I wish the so-called 'Iron Lady' every success. She advocates many sensible positions, like standing up to the Soviet Union, restoring family values and destroying the North. Most importantly, she would cut my Pa's taxes, which means more tuck for Boris!

Monday, 1st May

It seems my initial concerns were well-founded: old BoJo's standing at school has dropped precipitously since last term. This is partly due to Cameron Minor indulging in a whispering campaign against me. Apparently he claims I tried to put laxative in his coffee. What rot! The other factor is my time as opinion columnist for the *Chronicle*, during which I made some enemies. In retrospect, my piece about Snipes's bedwetting was not, perhaps, in the public interest.

The upshot of all this is I need to change the narrative: pull off a stunt so outrageous that it silences my critics. I spent a couple of hours this evening coming up with ideas. *Par exemple*:

- Fill Old Crighty's office with two dozen snapping turtles.
- Do a zip wire across the Thames, deliberately getting stuck halfway.
- Fake own death (desperate times call for desperate measures).

Eventually, I settled on a scheme brilliant in its subtlety. Simply put, I am going to sneak a load of beers into school and get everybody rat-arsed.

Tuesday, 2nd May

Initiated my plan (which I'm calling Operation Katzenjammer) this afternoon. Snuck into Adamsdale's, one of Windsor's less reputable newsagents, having artificially aged myself by drawing wrinkles on my face and putting flour in my hair. Carrying a couple of boxes of Watney's Red Barrel, I gingerly approached the counter. I was banking on old Mr Adamsdale being sufficiently senile as to not see through my disguise, and – hey presto! – the purchase was made with no request for ID.

Knowing I would likely be apprehended if I tried to bring the beer into school during daylight hours, I stowed the boxes in a bush near College. Around 2 a.m., I snuck out and – hyper-vigilant for beaks – brought the beers inside, hiding them under my floorboards.

Wednesday, 3rd May

Spent the morning very pleasurably, inviting the most prominent boys at Eton to a midnight soirée. Thrilled at the prospect of booze, all of them acceded to my demand for secrecy. I could feel my social cachet swelling as I made these invitations. Even Piers Davenant was impressed that I'd been so plucky as to sneak in alcohol.

'For a first year, you certainly have balls!' he said, accurately. 'Keep it up and you'll be a member of Pop, no question.'

Sometime after lights out, I found my humble room filled

with Eton's crème de la crème. There was Davenant and his Pop cronies, Edge-Llewelyn and Ridgeley-Watts, and Jessop-Jenkins, who didn't want to drink, but was keen to support me. Cracking open a Watney's, Davenant raised a toast:

'To Boris Johnson, a true Eton character!'

The group gave a subdued cheer, so as not to wake the beaks, and we all started tucking into our beers (I struggled not to wince at this unfamiliar taste). Just then, my door flew open and I found myself staring, in pant-wetting dread, at the vulturine face of Mr Crighton.

I would go into detail about the horrors that ensued, but, once again, my bottom hurts too much for me to continue writing.

Thursday, 4th May

A dark day, spent dealing with the fallout from last night. Naturally, we were all caned, but Crighton was particularly keen to discover who purchased the beer in the first place. Obeying the instinctive *omertà* of schoolboys, no one dobbed me in. However, as the boy whose room the beer was consumed in, I found myself the prime suspect.

Crighton told me: 'Just you wait until I can prove it was you that bought the beer. Given your shenanigans in Michaelmas and Lent, I wouldn't be surprised if you got sent down.'

I was utterly terrified. All of a sudden, I saw my plans collapsing before my eyes: no Eton, no Oxford, no bright future. I would be disgraced, robbed of my chance to climb the greasy pole to Great Man-dom. I retired to my room to rub my backside and plot my next move. Soon enough, a way out occurred.

I headed to Jessop-Jenkins's room. I hadn't been there before, as he had always come to me. We chatted a while about our aching arses, and then I made my request. Dominic stared at me, appalled.

'You – you want me to say *I* bought the beer?'

'You'd be doing me a tremendous service,' I replied. 'I'm on extremely thin ice as it is. I need someone to take the fall, or else my goose is cooked.'

The guy looked terrified and miserable. After a long pause, he lowered his head and spoke.

'Okay, Boris, I'll do it. After all, you are my best friend.'

Delighted, I clapped him on the back.

'There's a good chap!' I cried. 'And listen, you've no need to worry. Your record's clean as a whistle, so you shouldn't expect anything more than a rap on the knuckles.'

It turns out this wasn't entirely true. Jessop-Jenkins has been rusticated* for a week. Feel a little bad about that.

Friday, 5th May

Jessop-Jenkins was in a real state as he waited for his parents to pick him up.

'I've never heard them as angry as they were on the phone,' he lamented. 'They said I've let the family down horribly.' I told him his only crime was being a bloody good friend, and that, furthermore, I would write to him every day he was away, to keep him abreast of Eton gossip.

Saturday, 6th May

Rather lonely today. Edge-Llewelyn and Ridgeley-Watts have been drifting away for a while, and now no Jessop-Jenkins. He may be a weed and not really someone I consider my friend, but I suppose having him round isn't the worst thing.

---

* *Editor's note*: Suspended and sent home.

Sunday, 7th May

Was sitting on a wall, chewing a contemplative Curly Wurly, when Piers Davenant approached. He said that, even though our drinks had been busted by Old Crighty, the Pop boys remained impressed with my audacity.

'A bunch of us are going to hang out in my room and listen to the new Jethro Tull. We wondered if you'd care to join us.'

My heart thrilled at the prospect (of hanging out with them, not listening to prog rock).

> Those who for great power would vie
> To glorious Eton should hie.
> One's prospects will narrow
> If one goes to Harrow.
> And state school? You needn't apply.

Friday, 12th May

I've been hanging out with Davenant and the Pop guys rather a lot lately. You could say they've adopted me as a sort of mascot. As a result, I haven't been updating this diary, nor have I had much time to think about young Jessop-Jenkins. In truth, I'd forgotten he was back from rustication today, so was surprised when he stuck his head round my door. Strange as it is to say, he looked a fair bit older than he did a week ago.

'How are you doing, old chap?' I asked.

'Fine,' he replied. 'My parents wouldn't let me out of my room, so I was horribly bored. Didn't you say you were going to write me letters?'

'Hmm. Not that I recall.'

At this, Dominic shot me a sharp look, which I can't remember him ever doing before.

'Never mind,' he said. 'Why don't we go for a walk along the river, and you can tell me everything I missed.'

'Ah yes,' I replied. 'The thing is, I'm actually meant to be hanging out with Piers.'

'Piers?' he said, visibly stung. 'You're friends with *Davenant*?'

'Yes,' I replied, 'that beer stunt really did wonders for my reputation. I'd invite you along, but I don't want to ruffle any feathers with the Pop crowd.'

'I see,' he murmured, then left.

UPDATE: Something rather unsettling happened just now. Around one in the morning, I was shaken awake by Jessop-Jenkins.

'I'm a weed, am I?' he wailed. 'I'm not really your friend?'

I protested that I had no idea what he was talking about. By way of response, he brandished the book I'm currently writing in.

'You brushed me off earlier,' he said, 'so I wanted to know what you actually think of me. I snuck in here and I read your diary.'

At this point, the guy burst into tears.

'I knew you could be a rotter, but had no idea just how awful you are. You got me rusticated, and you still kept calling me names. Well, I may be a spineless wimp, but I promise you one thing: I will never forgive you for this.'

He dashed off, leaving me bleary-eyed and horrified.

Frankly, Jessop-Jenkins has no one to blame for this but himself. If he thought I was going to be his bestest buddy for life, then more fool him. As Petronius puts it in his *Satyricon, 'nomen amicitiae sic, quatenus expedit, haeret'* ('the name of friendship lasts just so long as it is profitable').

BORIS'S TEN RULES FOR LIFE

1. It's not lying if you don't bother to learn the truth.

Many people – politicians, for instance – make the mistake of going about laden with facts and statistics. However, when studiously ignorant of the aforementioned, one may argue one's case with total conviction. You might even be right, for all you know.

2. Be ridiculous.

You can't be caricatured if you're already a caricature. Whether they're laughing with or at you is irrelevant – just keep them laughing. It's better they think you a buffoon than know your true intentions.

3. The human back is a convenient place to store one's knife.

Loyalty is something we expect of others, not of ourselves. People are out to get you, so never pass up an opportunity for some healthy, vigorous backstabbing.

4. Do unto others, and then run away.

One tends to *suffer* the consequences, rather than, say, enjoy them. As such, I prefer not to be around when consequences turn up.

5. Never apologise.

Apologising is akin to presenting a lady with your severed ear: painful for you, and unlikely to be appreciated by the other party. 'If' is the ultimate get-out here, e.g. 'IF my setting fire to your mother caused you distress, then that's a shame.'

6. A friend is just an enemy you haven't yet made.

Some say there's no 'I' in 'team'. Well, I say you can't spell 'friend' without 'fiend'. No matter how dear your chum, bosom buddy or pal, you never know what sort of treachery they harbour inside. After all, there are many people who consider *me* a friend!

7. Always come top.

Whether it's a debate or a game of tiddlywinks, every interaction should be viewed as a fight to the death. If you are bested in any way, this will set in motion a chain of events leading to your humiliation and demise.

8. Consistency is for custard.

When addressing an audience, don't let yourself be constrained by what you told the last one. This way you can ensure support from both the Hungry Fox Association and Chickens Against Being Eaten.

9. Be a monstrous blancmange from Neptune.

That didn't make much sense, did it? Well, it wasn't meant to. I've discovered that often the best way to get out of a sticky situation is to make bizarre, irrelevant pronouncements. Your interlocutor is liable either to laugh or lose their train of thought.

10. Rules don't apply to me.

I am Boris and I can do whatever I want.

CHAPTER EIGHT

Consummatum est

Monday, 15th May

As grotesque as was Jessop-Jenkins's behaviour on Friday night, I must confess to feeling a modicum of guilt. It struck me that I might want to reconsider the way I treat others, as well as my attitude and general approach to life. Then it struck me, with even greater force, that I might *not* want to do those things. Still, I need to be distracted from these negative vibes, which is why I've signed up for the Debating Society. This is an Eton club that prepares one for the adult world, teaching one to speak confidently on subjects one knows nothing about.

Wednesday, 31st May

It turns out that your hero, Boris Johnson, is a genius at debate! I have excelled at every meeting I've attended, flitting between positions with ease and never actually answering a question. I realise now that my supposed vices (lying, showing off, constantly veering from the script) are virtues in the political arena. Who'd have thunk it?

Yesterday, I was inspired to write the following piece of doggerel, which I think is rather good:

HOW TO BE A GREAT DEBATER

Debating is a noble art,
Which in fair Athens had its start;
These days, the rhetorician's knowledge
Is mostly found at Eton College,
Where boys may learn, between their lessons,
Manoeuvres to persuade the peasants.
'Tis sensible, for you can bet
That some end up in cabinet.

So how might one the common throng
Ensorcel with a siren song?
The answer is a real no-brainer:
One must become an entertainer.
Facts may be challenged, claims assessed,

Which is, my friends, why it is best
To junk all that statistics crap:
The truth is but a booby trap.

Instead, when you're in some debate,
Address the listener like a mate.
I'm just a bloke, you should imply,
Not like that egghead other guy.
Make jokes, pull faces, wield a prop;
At random points, your thought-train stop
And cry: 'Oh lor, oh crumbs, egad!
I've quite forgot the point I had!'

Why be an evidence-based grafter
When you can win with gales of laughter?
The crowd now giggled to submission,
Impress on them the proposition.
If your opponent – dull and lame –
Asks you to justify some claim,
With made-up facts start bombin' 'em,
Then hurl a wild ad hominem.

Should they point out your facts are wrong
Do not back down, but, standing strong,
Say this: 'These quibbles idiotic
Reveal you as unpatriotic.
At our dear flag you've booed and hissed
And shown yourself a pessimist
By greeting fine plans with a frown
And always talking Britain down!'

The crowd goes wild and chants your name,
For you've won this debating game,
Not using logic, facts or reason,
But insults and a charge of treason.
That's how the world works, and our school
Equips us with these skills to rule.
Thus, being masters of debate,
We Eton boys keep Britain great!

Monday, 5th June

Received another missive from my incorrigible sis.

Dear blushing, buxom Borisina,

I was so pleased to receive your recent letter. I'm firmly of the opinion that we should maintain a frequent correspondence, as it's the only way you're likely to stay sane in that crest-filled hot-house. As someone who has spent their whole life around you, I know that, beneath all the bluster and bravado, you're really a kind, thoughtful, sensitive chap. Do hold on to who you are. I may tease, but it would be a huge shame if you were to change too much.

Yours with love,

Rachel

Humph. I suppose she means well.

Wednesday, 7th June

I continue to demolish my every opponent at the Debating Society. After today's meeting, the President took me aside and said that he'd never heard of a first year with such skills. He predicted that I would enjoy a bright future in politics. I confessed that I didn't mind the idea of being famous and giving speeches to vast crowds of supporters.

'What are you thinking,' he said: 'Labour, Tory or Liberal?'

I replied that I had no idea, as I had no real political convictions.

'Maybe that's not such a bad thing,' the chap replied. 'You may be able to use it to your advantage.'

Thursday, 8th June

Of course, despite my magnificent oratory, there's always a chance I might come a cropper. With this in mind, I spent today flipping through the codes and bylaws of the Debating Society. To my delight, I discovered that one can technically call any session to a halt, saving one from an ignominious defeat. The process is known as 'prorogation', which is a fancy way of saying 'to take one's ball and go home'. I shall have to remember this technique — it may well be of use in the future.

SPEECH TO THE DEBATING SOCIETY:
'THIS HOUSE BELIEVES THAT PUBLIC SCHOOLS ARE A BOON TO THE UNITED KINGDOM'

Mr Boris Johnson, speaking in favour of the proposition

(Approach the lectern, cheeks puffed out impressively, stooping slightly under the weight of what you're about to say. Clear throat at length.)

My honourable friends, members of the Eton Debating Society – good evening.

I must admit, I was surprised when given today's proposition. I was under the impression that this is a debating society, and yet here we are, discussing something unworthy of debate. The suggestion that the public school system does anything but enhance our nation is twaddle, utter bunkum, balderdash, tommyrot, piffle and fiddlesticks of the most insidious kind.

(Applause, cheers, cries of 'You tell 'em, Boris!')

Who can deny that our public schools provide a unique standard of education? They furnish our top universities, Oxford and Cambridge, with students of unquestioned academic rigour and excellent table manners. When these students come to enter the jobs market, they will bring with them highly practical skills, such as knowing Latin and Greek. What's more, the ex-public school boy is imbued with the strength of character that only separation from one's family and years of ritual abuse can provide.

(If you're losing them at this point, mess up your hair and mug for a bit.)

Where else can one find such scholastic and moral excellence? Comprehensives, where the only thing students learn is new stabbing techniques? These institutions are merely prep schools for prison. The teachers – barely more than ruffians themselves – cower under their desks, as feral youths wield coshes and flame-throwers. The average pupil is more likely to achieve an unplanned pregnancy than an O level. While we have use of our playing fields, the only exercise they get is running from the cops. Tell me, friends, would you like to be educated at such an establishment?

(Howls of 'No!' and 'I should bally well think not!')

Quite right. Compared to this fine place, any state school is a foetid hell-broth of blood, tears and excrement. Furthermore, I feel compelled to observe that my learned friend speaking against the proposition is a hypocrite. If he truly believes, as he claims, that the public school system is a net negative for this country, then why does he attend Eton College?

(Your opponent is knocked spark out by this rhetorical roundhouse kick. The crowd goes wild.)

My friends . . . My friends . . .

Should any of you still question the truth of our proposition, I would point to the conclusive evidence in this very room. That conclusive evidence is us. We are this country's future. We will be tomorrow's generals, tomorrow's judges, tomorrow's Prime Ministers. We will absolve the common people of the crushing responsibility to govern themselves. No matter how they vote, no matter what they do, we will be there, running the show. They may resent us, abhor us, call us inbred, chinless, silver-spoon-chomping poshos. But in the end, they know, deep down, that they need us. Some are born to be ruled. We, my friends, are born to rule. All we ask in return is to retain our immense wealth, and be pretty much above the law. For that service – for that sacrifice – the people out there should be eternally grateful. I yield the floor.

(*Bow deeply, basking in thunderous applause.*)

Young Boris is one of strong mettle;
The sort a wise fellow would bet'((
Achieve anything.   ---
He'd like to be King,
But for being PM he'd settle.

Friday, 9th June

With crushing predictability, Edge-Llewelyn and Ridgeley-Watts have come crawling back. Now that I'm a top debater and mates with Piers Davenant, they wish to hang out again. A more emotional type might tell them to sod off, but I've decided their friendship is tactically advantageous. The moment it's not, though . . .

'We hear you've shaken off that weed, Jessop-Jenkins,' said Ridgeley-Watts. 'Thank goodness we don't have to hang out with him anymore.'

I felt a pang of remorse, which I soon banished.

ETON COLLEGE
SCHOOL REPORT

STUDENT NAME: Boris Johnson   **HALF:** Summer

It affords me no pleasure to report that the situation has not improved since I last wrote to you. Indeed, I struggle to avoid the conclusion that Boris' behaviour has taken a distinct turn for the worse. When first I met Boris, I ascribed his occasional misdeeds to factors common for a boy his age: laziness, lack of curiosity, excess self-regard. Increasingly, though, I find myself detecting in him a cruel edge. He is capable of great fits of rage when denied some trophy he believes is his by right. At times, he seems thoroughly amoral, concerned only with self-advancement and petty displays of power. He is continually disloyal to those around him, but responds to any reciprocal disloyalty with wild self-pity.

I appreciate that these are serious charges to level at a thirteen-year-old. However, as Wordsworth observes, "the child is father of the man". What sort of man will Boris be, I wonder. The one suggested by his best traits: bonhomie, inventiveness, a desire to please others? Or one presaged by his worst traits: flippancy, slipperiness and untrammelled egotism? If my admonitions seem vague, I would draw your attention to the riot Boris caused in the Debating Society, as well as his setting fire to the playing field with a magnifying lens. While I currently lack the means to prove it, I strongly suspect he was involved in Dominic Jessop-Jenkins' recent disgrace.

I hope that Boris' subsequent years at this institution will instil in him a sense of responsibility, and a proper respect for the rules. As it stands, though, his primary characteristics are entitlement, effrontery and a love of his own voice. These attributes may serve him well one day, perhaps as an after-dinner speaker, or a contributor to light entertainment programmes on the wireless. However, if he ever aspires to a role entailing actual responsibility, then God help us all.

Yours ever,

James Parham

James Parham

Saturday, 24th June

The last day of term, and of my first year at Eton. Attended a meeting with Mr Parham, which, as I'd anticipated, was somewhat grisly. He spoke of squandered potential, disregard for others, etc. etc., blah-blah-blah. All of that seems quite irrelevant, especially given the momentous decision to which I've come.

I began this diary, nine long months ago, because I felt that future historians should understand the making of Boris Johnson. However, if I have learned anything at Eton, it is the value of opacity, of never breaking character or letting one's guard down. A magician, as they say, never reveals his tricks. Boris is my trick, and I intend to pull it off with aplomb. I don't want outsiders delving into my innermost thoughts and emotions – ideally, I wouldn't have any to begin with. For that reason, this shall be my final entry.

You may wonder, dear Diary, how I arrived at this decision. 'Why oh why,' I hear you wail, 'am I being made redundant?' Well, the deciding factor was this: I have realised what order of Great Man I am destined to be. I'm going to be Prime Minister. Here is my plan, which I sketched out over lunch:

- Join the Eton Society, aka Pop
- Balliol College, Oxford
- Bullingdon Club
- President of the Union
- Glamorous profession (journalist?), then politics
- Run through a few wives
- Mayor of London
- Senior cabinet position
- Number 10

My motto shall be 'Carpe Diem'
When one day I find myself PM.
I might start a war,
Move London offshore,
Or sell off the British Museum

The jolly splendid thing about being from the right background is knowing that these things will almost certainly come to pass. In terms of party, I suspect I'll be a Tory, but that's negotiable. Everything's negotiable. The only principle that can't be jettisoned is that Boris must win.

As I finish this, my last ever diary entry, I find myself

slipping into a dream. It's some time after the millennium, and there I am: older, stouter, but still recognisably the Boris beloved of Eton. I am standing outside the polished black door of Number 10, having been swept to power in an electoral landslide. Illuminated by the flash of myriad cameras, I wave to a crowd of supporters, who chant 'BO-RIS! BO-RIS! BO-RIS!' In every other part of the country, my clownish face and dishevelled hairdo are on newspapers, billboards, TV screens. I am loved. Or, if not loved, something even better: I am unavoidable. I fill up the whole world with my words, my jokes, my promises.

I turn and go inside, the iconic door closing behind me. Here I am. I have achieved everything I ever wanted. What do I do now? Well . . . I'm sure I'll muddle through.

Ave atque vale!

EPILOGUE

Where are they now?

As of this writing, BORIS JOHNSON MP is Prime Minister of the United Kingdom. However, the relentless opportunism with which he pursued that office has left him a hugely divisive figure. As Brexit threatens the economy, national security and the very existence of the UK, Boris is going to need some pretty good gags to get through this one.

RACHEL JOHNSON is an editor, journalist, television presenter and author. She publicly opposed her brother over Brexit, but still turned up to support him when he was made PM.

JACOB REES-MOGG serves in Johnson's cabinet as Leader of the House of Commons and Lord President of the Council. He hasn't got any less weird over the intervening years.

DAVID CAMERON blew up the country, then sauntered off to live in a shed, the ham-faced prick.

RUBELLA ST GEORGE attended RADA, then went on to pursue a career in acting, appearing in ITV dramas *The Sun Never Sets* and *Upton Manor*. In 2003, she married Russian oligarch Sergei Dyatlov, an outspoken critic of Vladimir Putin. The pair have not been seen since 2006, when Dyatlov's yacht mysteriously exploded.

JAMES PARHAM continued to teach at Eton until his retirement in 1999. He now lives in Provence and has repeatedly turned down requests to be interviewed about Boris.

ANDREW CRIGHTON died in 1985 of a rage-induced heart attack.

CHARLES CORKINGHAM-BLOUNT (now known as Charlie Cork) is Political Editor of the *Sun*.

DOMINIC JESSOP-JENKINS has, by all accounts, had a ridiculously good life. Emerging from his awkward teenage phase, Dominic's work as a male model soon took him to California. There he became fascinated with the emerging tech industry, heavily investing in a company called Apple. Today he is a fixture on the *Sunday Times* Rich List and is married to the actress Halle Berry.